ONE DAY FOR GOD

5-99

Alison,

How can I ever say thank you for petting FIRE into your impossibly full schedule? You are an inspiration to me and such a blessing to your families, always finding the time and energy to let the Spirit work through you.

Thank You!

Sally

One Day for God

A Guide to Your Own Retreat

ANTHEA DOVE

ABINGDON PRESS / Nashville

ONE DAY FOR GOD: A GUIDE TO YOUR OWN RETREAT

Copyright © 1996 by Abingdon Press

First published 1995 Triangle SPCK Holy Trinity Church Marylebone Road
London NW1 4DU

All rights reserved.

This book is printed on acid-free, recycled paper.

Library of Congress Cataloging-in-Publication Data

Dove, Anthea.
    One day for God: a guide to your own retreat/Anthea Dove.
       p.   cm.
    Includes bibliographical references.
    ISBN 0-687-01547-2 (pbk: alk. paper)
    1. Retreats—Christianity. I. Title.
BV5068.R4D67   1996
269'.6—dc20

95-39404
CIP

Scripture quotations, unless otherwise noted, are from *The Jerusalem Bible*, copyright © 1966 by Darton, Longman & Todd, Ltd. and Doubleday, a division of Bantam Doubleday Dell Publishing Group, Inc. Reprinted by permission.

Those marked NJB are from *The New Jerusalem Bible*, copyright © 1985 by Darton, Longman & Todd, and Doubleday & Company, Inc. Reprinted by permission of the publishers.

Those marked NRSV are from the New Revised Standard Version of the Bible, copyright © 1989 by the Division of Christian Education of the National Council of the Churches of Christ in the USA.

Those marked RSV are from the Revised Standard Version of the Bible, copyright 1946, 1952, 1971 by the Division of Christian Education of the National Council of Churches of Christ in the USA.

Those marked KJV are from the King James Version.

All quotations from the Psalms are from *The Liturgical Psalter* (Grail Version). Published separately as *The Psalms: A New Translation for Worship*, copyright © English text 1976, 1977, David L. Frost, John A. Emerton, Andrew A. Macintosh.

96 97 98 99 00 01 02 03 04 05 — 10 9 8 7 6 5 4 3 2 1

MANUFACTURED IN THE UNITED STATES OF AMERICA

This book is dedicated
with gratitude and affection to
Judy Howard, Colin Midlane, and
Patrick Stewart.

Contents

Acknowledgments

I would like to thank my editor, Rachel Boulding, for her consideration, cooperation, and sense of humor, and my husband, Christopher, for his support, encouragement, and long hours at the word processor.

Preface

One day within your courts
is better than a thousand elsewhere. (Ps. 84:10)

The writer of this psalm longs to be with God. He says:

My soul is longing and yearning,
is yearning for the courts of the Lord. (Ps. 84:2)

Would you like to take one day out of your life to spend with God?

Are you able to spare one day? Are you free to take one day to think and pray and walk with God?

If your answer to these questions is yes, then I hope this book will help you to commit yourself fully to that day and give it to God.

In one sense, of course, there is nothing that we can give to God, before whom we stand empty and powerless. God has given us everything: our lives, our world, our happiness, and the greatest gift of all, Jesus Christ. But we can, all of us, try to make a response to God in love, and one way of doing this is to give time for reflection and prayer. To set aside one day from our lives and make it a special gift to God is something many people can do. The purpose of this book is to help anyone who is willing to do this in their reflections on God, on themselves, and on the world we live in.

For a number of years I lived in the retreat center at Hengrave Hall in Suffolk, England. There I not only helped to run and give retreats, but was able to be on the receiving end of retreats given by others. It was an enriching experience from which I learned a great deal.

11

While I was at Hengrave I met a lot of retreatants. Some came just for a day, some for a weekend, some for seven or eight days. Some were very familiar with retreat making, needing no help or guidance from anyone. Others were just the opposite, drawn to spend time with God but desperately unsure how to go about it. All these people had two things in common: first, they could afford the journey to Hengrave and to pay for their keep (although no one would have been turned away for lack of money) and second, they had no dependents to keep them at home.

It seemed to me that there are probably many people who, given the chance, would like to make a retreat, but feel there is no possibility of getting away. There are also those who, whether at home or away, would not have the confidence to attempt a retreat on their own. And there are others, faithful seekers after God, who are always ready to explore new ways of coming close to him.

This book is an attempt to be of help to all such people. The retreat is planned for one day, but it is obvious that given the wide difference in experience, personality, and gifts of those who love God it may well take longer for some. Indeed, it may suit some people better from a practical point of view to take a whole week over the retreat, going through one chapter each day, or perhaps to divide it over a weekend.

When I began to write the book, I had in mind those people who had overwhelmingly busy lives, and for whom it will seem a mighty achievement to take just one whole day to be alone with God out of the turmoil of their everyday lives.

Ideally, the Preface and the Introduction to this book should be read a few days before beginning the retreat.

The day I describe has a clear structure. It is flexible and can be adapted to individual needs. In other words, there is a pattern and discipline to the day, which I hope will be a helpful guide. But how you use this structure is up to you, the retreatant. It is very important that if at any point you feel tired, overwhelmed, or stressed you should stop and take a break—relax into silence or go out in the fresh air—whatever feels right.

There is some suggested work in the retreat involving writing and drawing. Some people draw and write with ease; for others it is a real struggle. The writing in particular is important, but you are free to take your time over it. No one else will ever see it, unless you want them to, and there is no need to worry about spelling or punctuation or grammar.

Remember, everything in this day is optional. It is designed to help and encourage you. If something you are asked to do fills you with dismay, you do not have to do it. Even so, it may be worth a try! But perhaps the golden rule for the day is: Be gentle with yourself, even as God is gentle with you.

As with most things in life, it is easier for some than for others to take a day out. If you are in the hospital or in prison, for example, you may have plenty of time on your own and time to think, but because you are not a free agent you will not be able to give a complete, uninterrupted day. In such situations you may be able to find a way of adapting the book to your lifestyle.

If, on the other hand, you are at home, comfortably off and without dependents, it should be comparatively simple for you not only to take a day out but to go to a place that is specifically geared to your needs: a retreat house or a house of prayer, where you will be welcomed, fed in silence at the appropriate times, but left alone to spend time with God. The whole atmosphere of such places makes prayer and reflection relatively easy.

But unfortunately not everyone is free or able to go on retreat in this way. Some may find it a challenge and a struggle to carve even one day for God (or for themselves, as others may see it) out of their busy lives. Very often it is those who love God most and try hardest to follow Jesus who have the most action-packed lives, loving and serving others, depended upon by many people, regarded as indispensable. Yet those who are so busy in active work may well be the very ones who most need space in their lives for God.

If you decide to set apart one day for God, do not make the mistake of feeling guilty about it, of imagining that you are being selfish and abandoning those who need you. If your day goes well you will return refreshed, renewed, strengthened, and healed. You will be better equipped to love, to give, and to serve. Not only you, but those whose lives you touch, will benefit from your retreat.

The writer of Psalm 73 says: "To be near God is my happiness" (Ps. 73:28). This is true for all of us, for all the saints and sinners among us, for those of deep faith and for those who are seeking a meaning in life.

It is worthwhile then, to make the commitment of one day and seize it with enthusiasm. Thinking ahead to the day you will choose, you may like to read this extract from Sanskrit writings:

> Look to this day for it is life;
> the very life of life.
> In its brief course lie all
> the realities and truths of existence—
> the joy of growth,
> the splendour of action,
> the glory of power.
> For yesterday is but a memory,
> and tomorrow is only a vision,
> but today well lived makes every yesterday
> a memory of happiness,
> and every tomorrow a vision of hope.
> Look well, therefore, to this day.

There are of course, practicalities to be considered. Those people who have dependents, elderly parents perhaps or children, will need to find someone to take over their responsibilities, just for a day. They may also need to find a place away from home which does not cost money and where they can be alone. A minister, a priest, a good friend—one of these should be able to help with the loan of a room.

If you are one of those in this position of being lent somewhere for the day, of if you are using a familiar room at home, it is important that you make its atmosphere as conducive to reflection as you can. You will need to be warm, with a comfortable chair to sit on. A lighted candle (don't forget the matches!) or a flower and some taped music may help you at times. It is advisable to have with you a Bible, a notebook and pen, and perhaps some colored pencils. And please bring some small created thing like a stone, a shell, or a twig that you like. You will be invited to use this during the day.

The notebook is very important. When you use it, make certain that when you read it again you will understand what you have written and why you have written it. For example, if you are given a question and asked for an answer, write down the question as well as the answer.

You don't have to go without food during this day, though of course you can choose to fast. There should be no actual food preparation or cooking, other than boiling a kettle or heating up soup. Sandwiches made the night before, soup, fruit, and plenty of drinks should see you happily through the day.

The book is divided into seven parts to be used throughout the day, beginning before breakfast and ending before you go to sleep. Thus there is a clear framework for the day, but it is in no way rigid. It is meant to be a pattern for the reader to follow, but it is intended to be flexible. Readers will approach the day differently, according to their needs, likes, hopes, fears, and personalities!

The words "Do not be afraid" are said to occur 365 times in the Bible, and they are very appropriate here. Do not worry that you will ruin the day or not manage to do it well. In taking the first step of committing yourself to one day, whatever you make of it, you have given an offering to God.

Introduction

Does it seem like a crazy idea, to take a day off, not for a holiday or a rest, but to spend time with God? Perhaps you feel slightly foolish and self-conscious about doing such a thing? Perhaps your fellow Christians in your church manage quite well without undertaking anything so odd?

One person who found it necessary to take time out to be alone with God for several hours at a time was Jesus Christ. Mark gives us a picture of an exhausting evening in the life of Jesus. "That evening, after sunset, they brought to him all who were sick and those who were possessed by devils. The whole town came crowding round the door, and he cured many who were suffering from diseases of one kind or another" (Mark 1:32-34a). Then Mark goes on to tell us: "In the morning, long before dawn, he got up and left the house, and went off to a lonely place and prayed there" (Mark 1:35).

Jesus needed the refreshment that only God can give. How much greater is our need!

Like all worthwhile enterprises, a day set apart for God needs some preparation, apart from making sandwiches! We need first of all to want to be with God, to be able to pray with Richard of Chichester: "May I know thee more clearly, love thee more dearly, follow thee more nearly." We can spend some time in prayer for a few days before-hand. It may be helpful to identify with the writer of Psalm 63 in his intense desire for God, by reading these words very slowly and thinking about their meaning:

> O God, you are my God, for you I long;
> for you my soul is thirsting.
> My body pines for you

like a dry, weary land without water.
So I gaze on you in the sanctuary
to see your strength and glory.
For your love is better than life,
my lips will speak your praise.
So I will bless you all my life
in your name I will lift up my hands.
My soul shall be filled as with a banquet,
my mouth shall praise you with joy. (Ps. 63:1-5)

There is a good deal to ponder over in this psalm. You may prefer simply to dwell on the first four lines, and to read also the first two verses of Psalm 42:

Like the deer that yearns
for running streams,
so my soul is yearning
for you, my God.

My soul is thirsting for God,
the God of my life;
when can I enter and see
the face of God? (Ps. 42:1-2)

Yet however much we long for God, we cannot equal his longing for us. He is the faithful one, the one who waits for us, however long it takes, the one who will never give up on us. We may think that we have decided on this day, planned it and arranged it, but in truth we are simply accepting God's invitation, coming to the one who calls us.

It may be that, like the writers of these psalms, you are thirsting for God, longing to know him more, to understand him better, to discover yourself in relation to him.

It could be that this day that you are offering to God is exactly what you want. Very many people, especially today when life generally is so busy and so complex, feel an almost desperate desire to "get away from it all," to escape, even if it is only for the space of a day, from the rat race of their everyday lives. For them it is no hardship to seize a day to be on their own with God, to enjoy solitude and silence. They are the ones who can perhaps identify with the nun in Hopkins's poem, "Heaven-Haven":

> I have desired to go
> Where springs not fail,
> To fields where flies no sharp and sided hail
> And a few lilies blow.
>
> And I have asked to be
> Where no storms come,
> Where the green swell is in the havens dumb,
> And out of the swing of the sea.[1]

Such people are eager to be "out of the swing of the sea."

But others will approach the day differently. It may be that you are a lukewarm believer, or a doubter. Perhaps you stopped praying or gave up going to church long ago. Perhaps there are some things about God—the God of your understanding—that you simply cannot accept, not if you are true to yourself. Perhaps you have just been too lazy. On the other hand, you may be so overburdened with the cares and anxieties of your life that God and any sort of prayer life have been squeezed out altogether. You may be very conscious of your own sinfulness and feel that you are light-years away from anything to do with holiness and goodness. Or you may believe that you are just not good enough to tackle anything like this.

It is possible that none of these descriptions fits you and your state of mind. This does not matter. Every one of us is unique, every one of us will approach such a day in our own individual condition. But for those who can't wait, as much for the hesitant, it may be helpful to pause and look at some passages from Scripture. Some may speak to you more than others, depending on the way you are feeling at the moment.

To those who simply long to be with him, who thirst for him like a dry and weary land without water, God speaks in Isaiah:

> Oh, come to the water all you who are thirsty;
> though you have no money, come! . . .
> Listen, listen to me . . .
> Pay attention, come to me;
> listen, and your soul will live. (Isa. 55:1-3)

And John tells us that Jesus cried out, "If any man is thirsty, let him come to me!" (John 7:37).

Those who feel they are too burdened to spare a day may remember the words of Jesus in Matthew:

> "Come to me, all you who labor and are overburdened, and I will give you rest. Shoulder my yoke and learn from me, for I am gentle and humble in heart, and you will find rest for your souls. Yes, my yoke is easy and my burden light." (Matt. 11:28-29)

People ashamed of their sinfulness may take heart from these two readings, one from Isaiah and one from Jeremiah.

> "Come now, let us talk this over,
> says the Lord.
> Though your sins are like scarlet,
> they shall be as white as snow;
> though they are red as crimson,
> they shall be like wool." (Isa. 1:18)

> Return, faithless Israel, says the LORD. I will not look on you in anger, for I am merciful, says the LORD; I will not be angry forever. . . . Return, O faithless children, says the LORD. (Jer. 3:12-14 NRSV)

And for the doubters and hesitaters there is this passage from Deuteronomy:

> You will seek the LORD your God, and you will find him, if you search after him with all your heart and will all your soul. When you are in tribulation, and all these things come upon you in the latter days, you will return to the

LORD your God and obey his voice, for the LORD your God is a merciful God; he will not fail you. (Deut. 4:29-31a, RSV)

When you have read through these passages several times you may like to copy into your notebook a word or phrase that has a special meaning for you.

Remember, God is inviting you to share this day and will welcome you with open arms. There are no strings attached to our relationship with God, who loves us just as we are, in whatever condition that might be: sinful, weak, angry, depressed, fearful, hopeful, courageous . . . it simply doesn't matter.

One day, a few years ago, I went into a chapel to pray. There was only one other person there, also kneeling in prayer. When I got up to leave he followed me out, and I saw from his collar that he was a priest. He did not know me, but he said, "He is in love with you. He is holding your hand." Then he slipped back into the chapel.

I thought, "What a soppy thing to say! How extraordinary! What a funny man!"

It was only much later that I understood and accepted what that priest said to me. I got to know him and discovered that he was a no-nonsense, down-to-earth Irishman, full of life and humor, not "soppy" at all.

God *is* in love with me, with you, with every single human being.

In the writings of the prophet Isaiah, God speaks to Israel. Israel stands for all God's children and so for us. God says to Israel in Isaiah:

> As the bridegroom rejoices in his bride,
> so will your God rejoice in you. (Isa. 62:5b)

Please forget your reservations, take courage, say yes to God. This will be one day, your day, given to God.

CHAPTER 1

Dawn

Praying in Silence
Walking with God
Breakfast

The image of dawn is a very beautiful one. In Luke's Gospel, Zechariah compares Jesus himself to the dawn. In great joy at the birth of his son, he addresses the little child, who was to become John the Baptist, saying:

As for you, little child,
you shall be called a prophet of God the Most High.
You shall go ahead of the Lord
to prepare his ways before him.

To make known to his people their salvation
through forgiveness of all their sins,
the loving-kindness of the heart of our God
who visits us like the dawn from on high.
(Luke 1:76-78 Grail version)

Some people love getting up with the lark; for others it is always a real struggle to get out of bed. But this day is special, a day set apart, a day for God. So set your alarm clock for as early as you can bear, and begin your day in the quietest hours when most people are still asleep. It could be that you are already in the place where you are going to spend the day, or you may have to travel to it first.

You may like to begin by reading a piece of advice from a Native American. It may surprise you that in a Christian book I include a prayer from the people we used to call Red Indians and so wrongly thought of as savages. I would like to explain why this book contains one or two teachings from other faiths.

What Jesus asks of his followers is that we should love God and love one another. Part of loving is listening and being open. During this century, Christians of different traditions have become increasingly less suspicious and fearful of one another, more willing to listen and to learn. Jesus longed for Christians to be a light to the world, but for so long we have presented a puzzling divided picture of the church. Now, gradually, barriers are coming down, and all of us are beginning to see the riches within each tradition, to learn from one another.

An extension of this, of our calling to love, is to listen too to those of other faiths. The reason we often hold back from committing ourselves to this kind of openness is, at least in part, a good reason. It stems from our sense of loyalty to our own tradition, a deep conviction that what we believe is right. But it also stems from fear. We are afraid of looking at other faiths in case they somehow corrupt us or lessen our own commitment.

In fact what happens should be the reverse. If we approach Hindus, Muslims, Buddhists, Jews, and Native Americans in a spirit of love, our own faith will be greatly enriched. As a Christian, I would always hope that people of other faiths would come to know and love Jesus Christ, but I recognize too that there are aspects of my own faith that need developing. By studying the prayers and thoughts of people of other faiths I have learned much greater reverence for God's creation. I have also learned to value stillness and, most especially, the mindfulness that the followers of Buddha practice.

All the prayers or thoughts from other faiths that I have included for this day with God are perfectly in accord with the teaching of Jesus.

So here is the Native American's suggestion:

> When you arise in the morning,
> Give thanks for the morning light.
> Give thanks for your life and strength.
> Give thanks for your food.
> And give thanks for the joy of living.
> And if perchance you see no reason
> for giving thanks,
> Rest assured the fault is in yourself.

Giving thanks is certainly one of the best ways to begin any day. For myself, I like to say on waking the first two lines of Mary's song, the Magnificat:

> "My soul magnifies the Lord
> and my spirit rejoices in God my Savior."
> (Luke 1:47 NRSV)

Depending on the time of the year, you may be up before or after the dawn. Depending on the weather and the outlook from your room, you may be able to watch the sun rise. But whether or not you are aware of the movement from darkness to light, whether or not you have the pleasure of seeing the sky flushed with brilliant color, this is your dawn, your beginning in the adventure of this day. Now is the moment to seize the opportunity of using the whole day to discover more about God and about yourself.

There is a familiar saying: "This day is the beginning of the rest of your life." Of course this is true of every day, but its significance is much greater at this moment, because it is very likely that you will be changed in some way by the end of this day and your life may never be the same again!

Spending a day like this is an adventure, a challenge, a risk. There you are, an ordinary person (though nobody is "ordinary" in God's eyes) sitting in an ordinary room, about to embark on an exploration. You are not setting out in the steps of Columbus or Captain Cook, you are not venturing up the Amazon or aiming to conquer Everest, but you are undertaking something that may make a more profound impression on you than any of these experiences could, because you may find God in a way that you never have before.

There is something about the early morning, before we have broken fast, before the world outside comes alive, that for some people at least feels right as a time of prayer. Monks and nuns and many devout laypeople make a habit of rising early to pray. It is a good time to begin our day.

Praying in Silence

So there you are, alone and in silence. Make yourself comfortable, perhaps sitting in a chair or, if you prefer it, lying on the floor. You may like to light your candle. Light is a powerful symbol of Jesus, who said, "I am the light of the world," and so a lighted candle makes a good focus for meditation.

You may also like to play some quiet music. Some people would find this a distraction, interfering with the "music" of their silence, but for others it can be an aid to concentration.

Now you need to relax. First, relax your body. Sit or lie perfectly still. Become aware of your breathing, and breathe as deeply as you can. Then, one by one, very slowly and deliberately, tense each muscle of your body, including the tiny muscles around your eyes and mouth, and let it go. Begin with the top of your head and gradually make your way down to your toes, tensing and relaxing. It is very important not to hurry over this. If you are relaxing well, you may find yourself almost going back to sleep!

When you are ready, begin to listen. Whether there is music playing or not, there will be other small sounds that could interfere with your concentration if you let them; things like the sounds of traffic, of shouting in the street, a bird singing or a plane overhead. Listen intently to each one of these noises, and then let each one go, just as you let your tense muscles go.

And now we come to a much more difficult "letting go." You have begun your day with a lot of baggage—not sandwiches or your tape recorder or your candle—but the baggage of your deep anxieties and concerns. The more caring and sensitive you are, the harder it will be to shed these burdens. You may be worried about yourself. Perhaps you have a serious illness. You may be without a job. You may be badly in need of something. You may be lonely or bereaved or suffering from rejection in a broken relationship.

It may not be concerns about yourself that weigh you down. Many people suffer more for others than for themselves: a husband with a wife who is terminally ill, a mother with a son who is addicted to drugs, a daughter with a father sunk in depression. These are the ones who have an inkling of what it must have been like for Mary, the mother of Jesus, who had to stand at the foot of the cross and watch him enduring his agonizing death.

For parents, who have loved their child since birth, it can be a great sorrow to see him or her in pain, whether it is mental, physical, or emotional. Often the mother and father would do anything to help and find it hard to stand back, watching their son or daughter making grave mistakes. But our children do not belong to us. It is for them to make their own decisions, even when these seem wrong to us.

The poet C. Day Lewis wrote movingly about the need for children to go their own way:

DAWN

I have had worse partings, but none that so
Gnaws at my mind still. Perhaps it is roughly
Saying what God alone could perfectly show—
How Selfhood begins with a walking away,
And love is proved in the letting go.[1]

Whatever the nature of your particular sorrows, it may
seem too much to be asked to let go of them even for a
time. For some it may be impossible. But perhaps for a
short time you can try. Later in the day you will face your
suffering again, but perhaps for now you can make an
honest attempt to put it to one side. God knows you inside
out; he is aware of all that you carry, but the more pressing
your pain the more it will interfere with your concentration on God.

So you have tried. You have tried to relax in body and
mind. You have tried to let go of those things that overwhelm
you. You are able to say with the writer of Psalm 57:

My heart is ready, O God,
my heart is ready. (Ps. 57:7)

And like the prophet Isaiah who felt himself to be unworthy, you can say to God: "Here I am" (Isa. 6:9).

So what happens now? You are still, you are silent, you
are ready to be with God. How this is going to feel depends
on you, not on your willingness or your skill, not even
necessarily on your past experience, but on the sort of
person you are. Some people seem to have a natural,
childlike trust in God. For them, being in silence with God
is like basking in the sun or sliding into a warm swimming
pool where they float, gently buoyed up by the water.
Their eyes are closed, their cares drift away one by one and
everyday life is somehow suspended.

For most of us, coping with silence is rather more of a
challenge. It is not easy: the more conscientious we are,
the more we worry about the quality of our listening, and

praying, and this of course does not help us to attain a peaceful state of mind.

You will be spending a good part of the day in silence, because it is in being still with God that we can most hope to grow in God's likeness and deepen our understanding. So it is important not so much to "get it right," for it is hardly a question of that, but to be comfortable with the silence. The secret of this is at once simple and extremely difficult. The secret is to forget yourself.

After all, there is no need to be anxious about pleasing God. God is not a schoolmaster, not your boss, not like the sort of parent who demands your good behavior in return for love and acceptance. God loves you and welcomes you with open arms, just as you are.

So, if you can, just let go of yourself and your strivings, and let God take over. It may help to think of yourself as a child cradled in God's arms, or as a cup, open and receptive, waiting to be filled by God's peace and inspiration.

You will probably not be wholly successful. Even when you reach the end of this day you may find yourself struggling with silence. But remember, God is not counting your distractions, or making a note of your preoccupation with other things, or impatient because *you* are impatient, so it is a complete waste of time to be focused on these imperfections.

There is a paradox in the prayer of silence. I have suggested that you focus on God, that you relax in God's loving presence, but for most of us it is difficult for us to sustain this for long. Our minds may be fixed on God, but it is as though we are illumined by God's light to see ourselves more clearly. Being in silence can be rather like being stripped naked; one by one our self-deceptions fall away and our eyes are opened to weaknesses in ourselves that we had long forgotten or never even suspected. This can feel frightening, or even crushing.

If you are not used to silence, it is unlikely that you will be exposed to this anguish so early in your day. More probably, you will be plagued by distractions and find it difficult to concentrate. Do not fret about this; distractions only get worse the more you worry about them. You may like to think of the lines from John Greenleaf Whittier's hymn, "Dear Lord and Father of Mankind":

> Drop thy still dews of quietness,
> Till all our strivings cease;
> Take from our souls the strain and stress,
> And let our ordered lives confess
> The beauty of thy peace.[2]

However, if you are troubled by distressing revelations about yourself early in the day, firmly put them to one side and bring your silence to an end. We will be facing these problems later in the day.

There is no rule as to how long your silence should last. Again it depends on what feels comfortable. If you are not used to being in silence, a few minutes may well be enough. On the other hand you may feel a deep peace that you are reluctant to break. Don't break it!

> May we cherish the silence and not be afraid.
> May we know it not empty but full of Presence.
> May the Love at its heart calm our fears.
> May we know the gentle touch of a trusting hand.[3]

SILENCE

Although I have stressed more than once that there is no rigidity about this day, that it is for you to use as it feels right for you, there *is* a pattern laid out for you to follow. In each of the seven parts there will be some reflections for you to ponder over, at least one period of silence, a time for you to weigh up how the day is going, and an opportunity to do something practical like going for a walk or having a drink.

Your day is only beginning and it is possible that you are already unhappy. You feel sure that you cannot "do it right," that you are bound to be a failure. Please abandon this attitude at once, and resist all temptation to consider it again. You cannot fail, because failure is an impossibility on this day. There are no marks or medals. There is no Order of Merit with your name at the bottom (or top!) of the list. The day is simply your offering of yourself and your time to God, and it is up to God, not to you, what sort of day it turns out to be.

Walking with God

So there you are. You have "done" your silence; what happens next? There may be time for a walk. This could be an impossibility if it is pouring rain, or if you are in a wheelchair. In such cases you may have to fall back on your imagination.

A walk will refresh you and perhaps unstiffen those limbs that were supposed to be relaxed anyway! But more than this, a walk is a great opportunity for doing something that you may find yourself doing for the rest of the day and even for the rest of your life. A walk is a good way to begin "practicing the presence of God," that is, finding God in everything and everybody, being aware of God at some level of your being, relating to God in everything that happens.

My walk as I write has to be imaginary, like the walk of those who are kept indoors for one reason or another. When I step outside the freshness of the air revives me and I feel a surge of gratitude to God the Creator. I look up at the sky. I can see only a little patch of it because I am in a narrow street with tall buildings on either side, and what I see is a dull grey. But I rejoice, because the sky makes me think of heaven. I do not understand what heaven is or where it is. I am not even sure that it is a place. And yet to look upward is somehow to make a small act of worship. Men and women of different faiths and throughout our world have felt this down the ages. We believe in the sun and the moon and the stars when they are not shining. We believe in our God whom we cannot see, and somehow the narrow space of sky above my head symbolizes God's kingdom.

Then I look down, and what I see is very different. The pavement is littered with rubbish. I have to watch where I tread. I begin to make judgments, to resent the careless people who care nothing about the appearance of our streets, and the dog owners who are so irresponsible. Then I remember that I have no right to judge and no idea why people do the things they do. I think of an arthritic widower I know who lives alone and thinks the world of his dog. Probably he cannot manage to take Buster for a proper walk.

I pass an old woman. She looks miserable and tired and cross. I think about smiling at her, but thinking is as far as I get. My courage fails me, and now it is too late. I tell God that I am sorry for this feebleness, and reflect on my own timidity and self-centeredness that make me afraid to risk a rebuff.

On a newsstand outside a shop I see a headline: CHILD, THREE, MURDERED IN PARK. I feel horror, anger, distress, predominantly anger. Who could have done such a thing? I am intensely angry with the person who committed this dreadful crime, and with God for letting such things happen. I want to shout, "How *can* you?" It is all very well saying that this little child will now be safe and happy in heaven, but what about the pain and terror that she has had to go through? What about her parents?

At once I am brought up against the whole mystery of suffering, and as I gradually become calmer I recall my own convictions: that God does not cause suffering; does not interfere in the events of our lives; and is always there, in the heart of our grief. I believe God was there, with that little child, and is there, with the parents in their heartbreak. I pray for that mother and father, trying to imagine their unimaginable suffering, and then, with some reluctance at first, I pray for the murderer, who must surely be sick, and for those who love him or her.

I come to the park, a poor little park, small and flat and dusty, with no trees and, at this time of year, no flowers. I stand by the iron railings and look at the bedraggled, dripping bushes and the muddy paths. I look down on a puddle and see the colors of a rainbow. I stare, and my heart lifts in wonder. I think of all the hidden, unexpected things of beauty in God's world, and two lines of a poem come into my mind:

> A violet by a mossy stone
> Half hidden from the eye![4]

I think that there are always signs of hope to be discovered, however dreary our lives and our surroundings, only sometimes we have to look hard to find them.

On the way back to my room I see that the sky is lighter. I hear music blaring from someone's radio. It is not the sort of music I normally enjoy, but it is cheerful and tempts me to dance along the street. I am refreshed after my walk but glad to be back in my warm room again. I thank God for the walk, for what it has taught me, and I give thanks because I have a roof over my head.

Now it is time for *your* walk. When you come back, you may like to write about it in your notebook, perhaps underlining the times your mind turned directly or indirectly to God. You may like to study what you have written, and list what happened to you in relation to God. Here is such a list from my own walk:

- I felt grateful for fresh air and thanked God for it.
- I looked up at the sky and worshiped God.

- I felt angry and judgmental, then ashamed of my attitude.
- I became aware of my own cowardice and self-interest.
- I told God I was sorry for this.
- I was angry with God for "allowing" a small child to suffer.
- I thought about suffering and realized God's presence with all who sorrow.
- I felt a sense of wonder when I saw the "rainbow" in the puddle.
- When I heard music, I felt like dancing, a God-given joy.
- I felt thankful not to be homeless.

By now, especially if you have been out walking, you may be feeling hungry. But please make time before you eat for one more thing. Think about your experience of the past hour or so, and try to find a symbol that expresses how you feel. It might be a worm, a bud, a stone . . .

Write the name of your symbol in your notebook, and write it large:

If you like, explain your choice of symbol. And if you like, draw it!

Breakfast

For those who are not fasting, breakfast will be a welcome meal. It is never a good idea to eat quickly, or to swallow down your food as though it is a boring necessity.

God created the world and saw that it was good. Food, like all the good things of life, is given to us for our enjoyment. Of course, gluttony, greed, overindulgence—all these are sinful, but it is also sinful to treat our bread and marmalade and coffee as though they are of no account. It is not only that we should be aware of how blessed we are to be free from hunger. Food is good in itself, and should inspire us to gratitude and rejoicing.

The Buddhists have something to teach us about our attitude to the simple things of life:

> This cup of tea in my two hands—
> mindfulness is held uprightly.
> My mind and body dwell
> in the very here and now.
>
> When we drink tea in mindfulness, we practice coming back in the present moment to live our life right here. When our mind and our body are fully in the present moment, then the steaming cup of tea appears clearly to us. We know it is a wonderful aspect of existence. At that time we are really in contact with the cup of tea. It is only at times like this that life is really present.[5]

Sadly, grace before meals is seldom said or sung nowadays, but on this day we can give thanks to God each time we sit down to eat. It may suit you to use your own words, or to say this grace:

> Lord, I ask your blessing
> On me,
> On those I love
> On those who have no one to love them
> And on this good food.
> Amen.

CHAPTER 2

Early Morning

Solitude

Sin

Forgiveness

Thankfulness

Coffee

It is you whom I invoke, O Lord.
In the morning you hear me.
In the morning I offer you my prayer,
Watching and waiting. (Ps. 5:2b-3)

T his morning, after breakfast, you may be ready, like the writer of Psalm 5, to offer your prayer to God, to watch and wait for the movement of the Holy Spirit in yourself and in your life. But I suggest that you give yourself a break first.

There may well be times in the day when you need a break, even though it is not suggested. You may feel overwhelmed by the amount of material in the book, or the things you are asked to do. It is far more important that you are at peace with the day than that you "do everything." So break and rest whenever you feel the need.

This whole day is committed to God, but that does not mean that there should be no space in it for other things than concentrated prayer. God is present in every part of our lives: the trivial, the everyday, the physical, and the emotional aspects of it. And you, once you are committed to the pursuit of holiness, will be pursuing it in everything you do: in walking, eating, and relaxing as much as in praying. Very few of us can sustain a long, unbroken time of prayer, but this should in no way make us ashamed or fearful that we are somehow watering down the effectiveness of our day, by making time for other things. God may choose to "speak" to us when we are drawing, listening to music, knitting, carving in wood, or washing up. It may happen that we feel inspired more when we are engaged in such tasks than we do in the times we set aside specifically for prayer. We know that Jesus said,

> "The wind blows wherever it pleases;
> you hear its sound,
> but you cannot tell where it comes from or where it is going.
> That is how it is with all who are born of the Spirit." (John 3:8)

We understand this to mean that God the Holy Spirit is free to inspire anyone and everyone, no matter who they are or where in the world they live. He (some like to think of God's Spirit as "she") was never confined to the Jews, and is not confined to Christians or to any religious people. The Holy Spirit is entirely free. And so our God is free to influence, call, or inspire us whatever we may happen to be doing.

Be kind to yourself. Remember: you are not on an obstacle course or in a race. There is time in your day to rest, to have fun, just to "go blank."

Perhaps you may ask: "Then what makes this different from any other day?" There are three answers: first, you have made a commitment to keep it as a day specially set apart for God; second, the day is structured to help you; and third, you are in solitude.

Solitude

Solitude, like silence, can be difficult for those who are not used to it. Some of us—surrounded all day long at home and at work by people who make demands on our energies and emotions—long to be alone, only to find we don't really know how to cope with our own company!

Others spend a lot of time alone, and suffer from loneliness. Loneliness is something very different from solitude. It is a cause of misery to a great many people: the bereaved, especially those who have spent a lifetime in the company of someone they love, and those who for one reason or another find it impossible to make friends.

But solitude is a state of mind much desired by those who long to come closer to God. It is not a negation of life or of people: often its effect is to make us able to respond more sensitively and justly to our fellow men and women.

For Francis of Assisi, so active and tireless in his service of God and God's people, occasional solitude was of paramount importance. The place he loved more than any other, was Mount La Verna. This was a gift from Count Orlando of Chiusi who said, "I have a mountain in Tuscany which is very solitary and wild and perfectly suited for someone who wants to live a solitary life. It is called Mount La Verna. If that mountain should please you and your companions, I would gladly give it to you."[1] Even more gladly, Francis accepted this gift and transformed the mountain into a perfect setting for his mystical meditations. And in the last century Charles de Foucauld, who inspired the foundation of the Little Brothers and Sisters of Jesus, one of the most effective religious orders of all time, spent a long spiritual journey in solitude. He was a Trappist monk in France and Syria, a hermit in Nazareth, and a nomadic hermit among the Tuareg people in North Africa.

Nowadays a growing number of people believe they are called to the solitary life as hermits. You may not be among them, and you may well be thinking, "Francis and

Brother Charles were outstanding men, far removed from me in greatness and goodness." However, we can all seek to learn to value solitude, hoping it will bear fruit for us too.

Solitude, silence, stillness, and space: each of these is a gift to you on this day; each of these can deepen your understanding and enlarge your soul. It is in solitude, silence, stillness, and space that you are most likely to encounter God, and even if God chooses to meet you while you are writing or drying the dishes, it will be in the ensuing time of quiet and prayer that you will be able to savor what is revealed to you, keeping this treasure and pondering it in your heart as Mary did after the events surrounding the Incarnation (Luke 2:19).

After the break, you may go into another period of silence, sitting still and relaxed as before. These times of quiet with God are unique to you. No one else knows what happens or how you feel.

SILENCE

One effect on us of being alone with God, thinking about God and listening intently, is to become acutely aware of ourselves in relation to God, of our smallness and weakness and unworthiness. As we face our God and reach out, we long to be pure in God's sight, to be cleansed of all our sins.

Sin

Sin is a huge problem in all our lives. Often these days people, especially preachers, say that we seem to have lost our *sense* of sin. Certainly attitudes toward morality have changed, but perhaps not entirely for the worse. Sadly, it is often those who take a high moral stance with regard to sexual morality who are not only quick to condemn the people they consider to be immoral but sometimes actually find a prurient enjoyment in the failings of others.

They remind us of the Pharisees who seemed to want to condemn the adulterous woman:

> The scribes and Pharisees brought a woman along who had been caught committing adultery; and making her stand there in full view of everybody, they said to Jesus, "Master, this woman was caught in the very act of committing adultery, and Moses has ordered us in the Law to condemn women like this to death by stoning. What have you to say?" They asked him this as a test, looking for something to use against him. But Jesus bent down and started writing on the ground with his finger. As they persisted with their question, he looked up and said, "If there is one of you who has not sinned, let him be the first to throw a stone at her." Then he bent down and wrote on the ground again. When they heard this they went away one by one, beginning with the eldest, until Jesus was left alone with the woman, who remained standing there. He looked up and said, "Woman, where are they? Has no one condemned you?" "No one, sir," she replied. "Neither do I condemn you," said Jesus, "go away and don't sin any more." (John 8:3-11)

When we think about sin in general, or our own in particular, it is well to remember that the greatest sin is the failure to love. It is unhealthy to become obsessed with our own sinfulness and to mull despondently over a list of our shortcomings. All too easily we can become submerged in guilt, and this in turn holds us back from living free and fulfilled lives in the service of God. Sometimes it is more helpful to examine our consciences in a positive way, and to ask questions like this:

- Is my love genuine and sincere?
- Am I truthful with myself, with God, with others?
- Do I make a serious attempt to stand in the shoes of people who disagree with me?
- Am I generous?
- Am I quick to forgive?

- Am I aware of my own prejudices, with regard to race, sexuality, religion, social differences, intellectual differences, age?
- Am I cheerful?
- Am I a good friend?

Forgiveness

Many of us feel hopelessly weighed down by our sins. We believe we are unworthy, not fit to stand before God. You may believe that no one could be as wicked a sinner as you and that it is impossible for God or anyone else to forgive you.

But this is not so. Already in the Introduction to this book, you may have read the passage from Isaiah, where God says:

> Though your sins are like scarlet
> They shall be as white as snow. (Isa. 1:18)

and you may like to read this extract from Psalm 103:

> The Lord is compassion and love,
> Slow to anger and rich in mercy.
> His wrath will come to an end;
> he will not be angry for ever.
> He does not treat us according to our sins
> nor repay us according to our faults.
> For as the heavens are high above the earth
> so strong is his love for those who fear him.
> As far as the east is from the west,
> so far does he remove our sins.
> As parents have compassion on their children,
> the Lord has pity on those who fear him. (Ps. 103:8-13)

These passages from the Old Testament are not just colorful pieces of ancient poetry. They speak the truth and they are just as true, today, for you. Yet it is very hard to

convince people of this. Jesus himself wanted his hearers to
know, to believe in their hearts that God will forgive even
the most wicked and evil of us. And so, he told them a story,
recorded in Luke 15, the parable of the prodigal son.

> "A man had two sons. The younger said to his father,
> 'Father, let me have the share of the estate that would come
> to me.' So the father divided the property between them.
> A few days later, the younger son got together everything
> he had and left for a distant country where he squandered
> his money on a life of debauchery.
>
> When he had spent it all, that country experienced a
> severe famine, and now he began to feel the pinch, so he hired
> himself out to one of the local inhabitants who put him on
> his farm to feed the pigs. And he would willingly have filled
> his belly with the husks the pigs were eating but no one
> offered him anything. Then he came to his senses and said,
> 'How many of my father's paid servants have more food than
> they want, and here I am dying of hunger! I will leave this
> place and go to my father and say: Father, I have sinned
> against heaven and against you; I no longer deserve to be
> called your son; treat me as one of your paid servants.' So he
> left the place and went back to his father.
>
> While he was still a long way off, his father saw him and
> was moved with pity. He ran to the boy, clasped him in his
> arms and kissed him tenderly. Then his son said, 'Father,
> I have sinned against heaven and against you. I no longer
> deserve to be called your son.' But the father said to his
> servants, 'Quick! Bring out the best robe and put it on him;
> put a ring on his finger and sandals on his feet. Bring the
> calf we have been fattening, and kill it; we are going to have
> a feast, a celebration, because this son of mine was dead
> and has come back to life; he was lost and is found.' And
> they began to celebrate." (Luke 15:11-24)

This is probably a very familiar story. You may well have
heard it or read it a hundred times. Yet it is a story that
holds such depth of meaning that we can go on learning
from it and being moved by it. For me it is one of the

greatest stories of all time, and the painting in which Rembrandt captures its essence is one of the greatest paintings.

Let us try then to look at the story with fresh eyes. The younger son represents us, you and me and all sinners. He plunges deeply into sin of the worst kind. First of all he shows greed: the excessive love of money which is the downfall of so many people, leading them into a spiral of unscrupulousness where material success becomes the be-all and end-all of their lives. When we look carefully at the causes of war, violence, and poverty in the world we find so often that the root cause for all these things is greed for money. Those who make money out of the arms trade, together with the multinational organizations and the banks who exploit the helplessness of people in poor countries, stand in great need of forgiveness.

We may feel indignant at their behavior and thankful not to be like them, in much the same way as the Pharisee looked on the publican in Luke 18:11: "I thank you, God, that I am not grasping, unjust, adulterous like the rest of mankind, and particularly that I am not like this tax collector here."

Yet we too bear some of the guilt for the exploitation of our weaker brothers and sisters if we are content to sit back and allow these things to go on in our world.

Money in itself is not evil. It is useful and necessary. Nor is it a sin to be rich, especially when the wealthy spend their money with wisdom and generosity. But the young man in the story was sinful in that he was greedy and grasping, wanting the money to spend on his own pleasure.

Does all this seem irrelevant to you? Perhaps at this point you can see no resemblance between you and the younger son, especially if you have to struggle to make both ends meet. Others may have a choice about how they spend their money. I think many people have a problem with this: they feel compassion for those in need and they are uncertain about how much to give. They want to be generous and they are not sure how far to go in doing without things they need, like, or want for themselves. This is a dilemma common to everyone who cares about her or his neighbor, and it is never easy to hold the balance between indifference and overscrupulousness.

Let us go back to the younger son. As soon as he got his hands on the money he was off. He had no thought for how his father or his brother might feel. He was entirely bent on his own concerns, his own gratification. In other words, he was thoroughly selfish.

I imagine there are some saintly people in our world, and perhaps Mother Teresa is one of them, who live completely unselfish lives with no thought for their own welfare or happiness. However, nearly every single one of us *is* selfish, to a greater or lesser degree, at some time or other in our lives, and it is probably true to say that most of us are selfish for a lot of the time. Sometimes it is hard not to despair about this. For me it is the battle of a lifetime, fighting against my self-interest. And when I pause to examine my conscience, to think where I am going wrong in my journey as a Christian, I am sometimes shocked to realize how much I am preoccupied with my own concerns and how far I am from becoming selfless.

It does help to be married, or to live with someone you love, because then you can train yourself to put the other person first and do it gladly. In theory at least, it should help even more to live with a group of others in a community. I tried this for over four years, and I well remember one incident at the beginning.

Eight of us were sitting around the table at supper, and a bowl of fruit was put in front of us. I saw that there were two apples, two bananas, two oranges, and two peaches. How I longed for a peach! But I was at the wrong end of the table. I watched as each person stretched out his or her hand, and I willed them not to take a peach. But of course, two people did, and I was left with a rather moldy orange. Afterward I reflected with shame on this incident, aware that a truly good person would have hoped that others would enjoy the peaches.

We are all human, we are not angels, we are by no means perfect. It follows that sometimes we will be self-centered, will "put Number One first." But it is as well to be wary and keep a watch on ourselves, realizing that wholehearted love demands selflessness.

In recent years there has been a growing emphasis on self-fulfillment, especially for women. This is an excellent and much needed development, provided we don't get so carried away with the pursuit of our own freedom and potential that we fail to realize what the effects of this may be on others. It is not part of God's plan or dream for any of us that we should become doormats for others to walk over; neither is it reasonable that in the search for our own fulfillment we should disregard the hopes and rights of the people whose lives we touch.

I once met a vicar who loved his work in an inner city, where he was active in serving the poor. His children had grown up and his wife had successfully studied to become a teacher of disabled children. She was offered a job in a quite different part of the country, a prosperous suburban area, and she very much wanted to accept it. The vicar could not bear the idea of leaving his parish. He was distressed and wanted to talk about his problem, while realizing that only he and his wife could find a solution. I wonder what decision they reached.

Again let us return to Jesus' parable. The younger son went on to sin in earnest. He "*squandered* his money on a life of *debauchery*" or, as the King James Version has it, "*he wasted his substance* with *riotous living*" [my italics]. Strong words, either way!

Evidently he was thorough in his sinning, guilty of abandoning himself to serious wrongdoing. Most of the people I know, and probably those you know, are not like that. In their own eyes and the eyes of their friends they are relatively good people. They are faithful in marriage, law-abiding citizens, never guilty of violence or stealing, often regular churchgoers. But we have to remember that if we fit into this category, we are still likely to be sinners in ways that are not especially colorful or dramatic, but nevertheless loveless. Righteous people can too easily become *self*-righteous and unaware of their lack of tolerance, charity, and open-mindedness.

Many of us may be more conscious of our guilt and sin because what we have done or are doing is flagrantly wrong. Adultery, even in these permissive days, is generally regarded as sinful, and there are many grievous sins such as rape, murder, or the sexual abuse of children that society finds it hard to pardon and we would find even harder to pardon in ourselves. Some men and women are so overburdened with guilt and horror at what they have done that they dare not confess it to anyone. They feel themselves to be beyond acceptance, outside forgiveness.

When he finally made up his mind to go home, the younger son in Jesus' story was in a similar state. He bitterly regretted what he had done, and was ashamed in the depths of his being. He did not go home hoping for acceptance and forgiveness, but quite simply because he was starving.

So how did his father, who in the story represents God our Father, react? In the same way that God reacts to all of us who return in shame and regret, whatever we have done, with welcoming and rejoicing.

In the story Jesus told, the old man does not just wait for his repentant son with open arms; he actually runs to meet him, clasps him in his arms, and kisses him tenderly. It is important to remember this, so that when we approach our God in a spirit of true repentance, we will not be fearful, but answer God's joyful, loving response with our own joy and love.

Perhaps you feel you need to pause now, and use this time of silence to think about yourself and your failings, taking an honest look at the state of your soul. Never forget that *no one* is beyond redemption. God forgives all who are truly sorry.

SILENCE

Now you may like to pray through this extract from Psalm 51:

Have mercy on me, God, in your kindness.
In your compassion blot out my offense.
O wash me more and more from my guilt
and cleanse me from my sin.

My offenses truly I know them;
my sin is always before me.
Against you, you alone have I sinned;
what is evil in your sight I have done.

Indeed you love truth in the heart;
then in the secret of my heart teach me wisdom.
O purify me, then I shall be clean;
O wash me, I shall be whiter than snow.

Make me hear rejoicing and gladness
that the bones you have crushed may thrill.
From my sins turn away your face
and blot out all my guilt.

A pure heart create for me, O God,
put a steadfast spirit within me.
Do not cast me away from your presence,
nor deprive me of your holy spirit.

Give me again the joy of your help;
with a spirit of fervor sustain me. (Ps. 51:1-4*a*, 6-12)

Every one of your sins is completely washed away. God has forgotten them. So can you. You are forgiven, reconciled with God. God has forgiven you; you are blessed and on the way to healing and peace of mind.

Thankfulness

Your heart may overflow with thankfulness and you may be happy to pray the beginning of Psalm 138:

I thank you, Lord, with all my heart,
you have heard the words of my mouth.
In the presence of the angels I will bless you.
I will adore before your holy temple.

I thank you for your faithfulness and love
which excel all we ever knew of you.
On the day I called, you answered;
you increased the strength of my soul. (Ps. 138:1-3)

When you have rested awhile, try to think of a symbol that expresses how you feel now, and write its name in your notebook. It might be clear water, a bird flying, a happy child . . .

• Can you explain your symbol?
• Can you draw it?

Coffee

This has been an intense time of reflection and prayer and you will need a break. It should be good to move around, do aerobics or some gentle exercises, dance, or go for a short walk. Then you can relax with a cup of tea or coffee.

CHAPTER 3

Late Morning

God the Father and Creator
God the Holy Spirit
Lunch

Alleluia!
I love the Lord for he has heard
the cry of my appeal;
for he turned his ear to me
in the day when I called him. (Psalm 116:1-2)

You began, very early this morning, in a silence where you tried to let go of your worries and shift your concentration from yourself to God. Later, you have been encouraged to think about your sins and ask for forgiveness for them.

It could be that you are still not at peace. So much looking inward can sometimes lead to frightening revelations about ourselves, things we never expected, a sort of chaos and darkness. These things are very complex as well as unnerving, and we may even need professional help to deal with them. There are times in all our lives when we could benefit not just from a shoulder to cry on but from the help of an experienced counselor.

If you are in this situation the best thing you can do now is to resolve to find a spiritual director (most of them prefer to be called soul friends) or a Christian counselor as soon as possible. In the meantime, remember how often in the Bible God has said "Do not be afraid," and give yourself in complete trust to him. God knows the secrets of your heart, about the darkness and confusion, and God loves you.

Now you can go back to silence; healed, restored, forgiven, with your eyes fixed on God as the single focus of your prayer. Keep looking toward God. The prophet Isaiah says:

> Thou dost keep him in perfect peace,
> whose mind is stayed on thee. (Isa. 26:3 RSV)

May this experience of peace in the Lord's presence be yours too.

SILENCE

God the Father and Creator

We know that our God is a trinity of three persons, God the Father, God the Son, and God the Holy Spirit. This is acknowledged to be a mystery, beyond human understanding. This book is not concerned with the Trinity as doctrine. After all, our God is wholeness itself. But we relate to God in different ways at different times.

Jesus himself speaks of the three aspects of God. At the end of Matthew's Gospel we have this account:

Meanwhile the eleven disciples set out for Galilee, to the mountain where Jesus had arranged to meet them. When they saw him they fell down before him, though some hesitated. Jesus came up and spoke to them. He said, "All authority in heaven and on earth has been given to me. Go, therefore, make disciples of all the nations; baptize them in the name of the Father and of the Son and of the Holy

Spirit, and teach them to observe all the commands I gave you. And know that I am with you always; yes, to the end of time." (Matt. 28:16-20)

It is usual to speak of God as the first person of the Trinity, Jesus as the second, and the Holy Spirit as the third. But in this book we are going to look at God first and the Holy Spirit second, because much more time will be devoted to Jesus.

The reason for this is that Jesus is the most "accessible" to us. He is the one we know most about, and the one who is most like us. So far on this day our thoughts about God have been about God's unconditional love for us, something we can never emphasize enough because for so many of us it is hard to grasp.

There are people who have never known what it is like to be loved even as small children, and for them it is extremely difficult to believe in a loving God. Most of us will have had at least some experience of love, however imperfect, at an early age; but as we grow up and grow older we become increasingly aware of our own unlovable qualities, and find it hard to accept that God, who knows us through and through, loves us just as we are. If you are not completely confident about this, it may help you to read this passage from Isaiah and take it to heart:

> Shout for joy, you heavens; exult, you earth!
> You mountains, break into happy cries!
> For the Lord consoles his people
> and takes pity on those who are afflicted.
>
> For Zion was saying, "The Lord has abandoned me,
> the Lord has forgotten me."
> Does a woman forget her baby at the breast,
> or fail to cherish the son of her womb?
> Yet even if these forget,
> I will never forget you.

See, I have branded you on the palms of my hands.
(Isa. 49:13-16*a*)

These are reassuring words for those who sometimes find themselves unable to trust, or unable to feel God's comforting presence.

And it is not only in the Old Testament that we find reassurance about the love of God. It is generally believed that John who wrote the Gospel is John who was the "disciple Jesus loved." At the end of his life, when he was a very old man, he seems to have increasingly come to believe that love is the only thing that matters. Here is an extract from his first letter:

> My dear people,
> let us love one another
> since love comes from God
> and everyone who loves is begotten by God and knows God.
> Anyone who fails to love can never have known God,
> because God is love.
> God's love for us was revealed
> when God sent into the world his only Son
> so that we could have life through him;
> this is the love I mean:
> not our love for God,
> but God's love for us when he sent his Son
> to be the sacrifice that takes our sins away.
> My dear people,
> since God has loved us so much,
> we too should love one another. (1 John 4:7-11)

Recently I listened to this story in a sermon: "A guy who was only four feet tall was going out with a girl who was six feet tall. They were walking home from the pub when the guy plucked up his courage and asked the girl if he could kiss her. When she said 'Yes,' he heaved a great boulder, which happened to be lying on the roadside, in front of him, climbed onto it and kissed the girl. Then they

51

continued on their way. It was about a mile to the girl's home and when they got to her doorstep, the guy asked if he could kiss her again. This time the girl said 'No!'

" 'You mean I've carried this boulder all this way for nothing!' the guy exclaimed."

It is a silly story, and it is not to be taken too literally! But it has a powerful moral. The point is that in order to be loved by God, you do not have to carry any boulders; you do not have to *do* anything at all. So often we are caught up with the idea of *earning* God's approval or love. We feel that we have to be good and do our *duty*, duty that Wordsworth called, "Stern daughter of the voice of God."[1] It is not God who is stern. He does not ask us to be dutiful, only to respond freely and gladly to his love.

God is your Father, our Father. God loves us so much that he gave his only Son to come and live on earth among us and to die a most cruel death so that we might be redeemed.

> All people clap your hands,
> cry to God with shouts of joy!
> For the Lord, the Most High, we must fear,
> Great King over all the earth. (Ps. 47:1-2)

God who loves each one of us so intimately and tenderly is also the Holy One, the Lord of the Universe, mysterious and wonderful—both Abba (Dad), who cradles us in his arms, and Yahweh (the Lord), before whom we kneel in adoration.

In the Old Testament there are many references to the awesomeness of God. Moses, the simple shepherd, is changed forever after this encounter:

> Moses was looking after the flock of Jethro, his father-in-law. He led his flock to the far side of the wilderness and came to Horeb, the mountain of God. There the angel of the Lord appeared to him in the shape of a flame of fire, coming from the middle of a bush. Moses looked; there was

the bush blazing but it was not being burnt up. "I must go and look at this strange sight," Moses said, "and see why the bush is not burnt." Now the Lord saw him go forward to look, and God called to him from the middle of the bush. "Moses, Moses!" he said. "Here I am" he answered. "Come no nearer" he said. "Take off your shoes, for the place on which you stand is holy ground. I am the God of your father," he said, "the God of Abraham, the God of Isaac and the God of Jacob." At this Moses covered his face, afraid to look at God. (Exod. 3:1-6)

Before God we stand in awe, aware of our smallness and insignificance. We acknowledge God's greatness and majesty.

Many of us have felt a sense of awe, of the majesty and wonder of God, at different moments of our lives. Sometimes this happens when we visit a great cathedral and look up at the soaring arches, or toward a brilliant stained glass window that seem in themselves to proclaim the glory of God. Or we may be moved to praise and adoration by something simpler: a field blazing with poppies, a child sleeping, the nobility of the human spirit manifested in people like Gandhi or Mandela—all such things can lift our hearts in worship of our God. Perhaps for most of us it is usually nature that inspires us to glorify the Lord. Such was the case with the writer of Psalm 93:

> The Lord is King, with majesty enrobed;
> the Lord has robed himself with might,
> he has girded himself with power.
>
> The world you made firm, not to be moved;
> your throne has stood firm from of old.
> From all eternity, O Lord, you are.
>
> The waters have lifted up, O Lord,
> the waters have lifted up their voice,
> the waters have lifted up their thunder.

Greater than the roar of mighty waters,
more glorious than the surgings of the sea,
the Lord is glorious on high.

Truly your decrees are to be trusted.
Holiness is fitting to your house,
O Lord, until the end of time.

We often describe God as almighty, all-powerful, omnipo-
tent. I find this a difficult concept. I do believe that God
is all-loving. I believe that God's love and compassion are
far greater than any human being can feel. It follows that
when God sees injustice and suffering and evil of any kind,
he must long to intervene. The fact that he does not must
mean that he cannot.

The forces of evil are a terrible power in our world.
Sometimes, for some of us, the kingdom of God may be
within us, but the perfection of the kingdom has not yet
come. God's reign is not yet established. One day Isaiah's
prophecy will come true, when:

The wolf lives with the lamb,
the panther lies down with the kid,
calf and lion cub feed together
with a little boy to lead them.
The cow and the bear make friends,
their young lie down together.
The lion eats straw like the ox.
The infant plays over the cobra's hole;
into the viper's lair
the young child puts his hand.
They do no hurt, no harm,
on all my holy mountain,
for the country is filled with the knowledge of God
as the waters swell the sea. (Isa. 11:6-9)

But that time has not yet come. Our God, our Father, our
Creator, can only suffer with us. God is vulnerable rather

than powerful, siding with the poor, the weak, the oppressed. "The Lord is close to the broken-hearted" (Ps. 34:19). God is present with all of us when we suffer.

SILENCE

> By the words of the Lord his works come into being
>   and all creation obeys his will.
> As the sun in shining looks on all things,
>   so the work of the Lord is full of his glory.
> (Ecclus. 42:15-16)

God is also our Creator. There is a wonderful, joyful psalm written in praise of the Lord for creation. It is a very long psalm; you may like to read it through slowly, taking your time and making it your own song of praise and adoration and thankfulness.

> Bless the Lord, my soul!
> Lord God, how great you are,
> clothed in majesty and glory,
> wrapped in light as in a robe!
>
> You stretch out the heavens like a tent.
> Above the rains you build your dwelling.
> You make the clouds your chariot,
> you walk on the wings of the wind;
> you make the winds your messengers
> and flashing fire your servants.
>
> You founded the earth on its base,
> to stand firm from age to age.
> You wrapped it with the ocean like a cloak:
> the waters stood higher than the mountains.
>
> At your threat they took to flight;
> at the voice of your thunder they fled.
> They rose over the mountains and flowed down

to the place which you had appointed.
You set limits they might not pass
lest they return to cover the earth.

You make springs gush forth in the valleys;
they flow in between the hills.
They give drink to all the beasts of the field;
the wild asses quench their thirst.
On their banks dwell the birds of heaven;
from the branches they sing their song.

From your dwelling you water the hills;
earth drinks its fill of your gift.
You make the grass grow for the cattle
and the plants to serve our needs,
that we may bring forth bread from the earth
and wind to cheer our hearts;
oil, to make our faces shine
and bread to strengthen our hearts.

The trees of the Lord drink their fill,
the cedars he planted on Lebanon;
there the birds build their nests;
on the treetop the stork has her home.
The goats find a home on the mountains
and rabbits hide in the rocks.

You made the moon to mark the months;
the sun knows the time for its setting.
When you spread the darkness it is night
and all the beasts of the forest creep forth.
The young lions roar for their prey
and ask their food from God.

At the rising of the sun they steal away
and go to rest in their dens.
Men and women go out to their work,
to labour till evening falls.

How many are your works, O Lord!

In wisdom you have made them all.
The earth is full of your riches.

There is the sea, vast and wide,
with its moving swarms past counting,
living things great and small.
The ships are moving there
and the monsters you made to play with.

All of these look to you
to give them their food in due season.
You give it, they gather it up;
you open your hand, they have their fill.

You hide your face, they are dismayed;
you take back your spirit, they die,
returning to the dust from which they came.
You send forth your spirit, they are created;
and your renew the face of the earth.

May the glory of the Lord last for ever!
May the Lord rejoice in his works!
He looks on the earth and it trembles;
the mountains send forth smoke at his touch.

I will sing to the Lord all my life,
make music to my God while I live.
May my thoughts be pleasing to him.
I find my joy in the Lord.

Bless the Lord, my soul. (Ps. 104:1-34, 35b)

Which is your favorite verse in this psalm? I think mine
is the one about the rabbits hiding in the rocks. In your
notebook, if you can, write a verse of your own to add to
the psalm.

You may like now to reflect on the things you find
wonderful and this in turn may make you long to recap-
ture your own sense of wonder.

SILENCE

While I have been writing this book I have had a spell of illness during which I was able to do nothing except sit in my chair. In some ways, of course, this was limiting and frustrating, but one consolation lay in thinking about the loveliness of nature and all the beauty I have seen and heard and experienced.

In his well-known poem "Daffodils," Wordsworth describes the host of golden daffodils he came upon, "fluttering and dancing in the breeze." He goes on to say that he will go on recalling the sight of them long after this day. When he is lying on his couch "in vacant or in pensive mood" the daffodils will

> flash upon that inward eye
> Which is the bliss of solitude.[2]

Well, here you are in solitude, too. Your inward eye is open to see, your inward ear to hear. Allow yourself to enjoy again those delights of God's world that you have known in the past. You may like to make a list of some of them in your notebook. It could read something like this:

- seeing the first snowdrop
- standing under a waterfall
- gazing up at the moon
- listening to a clarinet quintet
- looking at a city canal, transformed in sunlight
- hearing a blackbird singing after rain
- smelling coffee or new-mown grass
- watching children play
- tasting fresh raspberries
- swimming in the sea
- feeling the wind in my face

All through the ages, people have been writing and making music and painting and sculpting in praise of God the Creator. I have chosen two examples of the thoughts of two women which I find inspiring. I hope you will too.

Hildegarde of Bingen was a very gifted nun who lived in Germany in the twelfth century. Her writings speak to us today.

> Glance at the sun. See the moon and the stars.
> Gaze at the beauty of earth's greenings.
> Now, think.
> What delight God gives to humankind with all these things . . .
> All nature is at the disposal of humankind
> We are to work with it. For without it we cannot survive.[3]

Mother Julian was a hermit who lived in Norwich, England in the fourteenth century. During a severe illness, she saw visions which she called "shewings of our Lord." For twenty years she meditated on these, and then she wrote them down under the heading *Revelations of Divine Love*.

This short extract from the writings of Julian gives us some idea of how she understands God and how real God is to her.

> He showed me a little thing, the size of a hazelnut, in the palm of my hand, and it was as round as a ball. I looked at it with my mind's eye and I thought, "What can this be?" An answer came, "It is all that is made." I marvelled that it could last, for I thought it might have crumbled to nothing, it was so small. And the answer came into my mind, "It lasts and ever shall because God loves it." And all things have being through the love of God.
>
> In this little thing I saw three truths. The first is that God made it. The second is that God loves it. The third is that God looks after it.
>
> What is he indeed that is maker and lover and keeper? I cannot find words to tell.[4]

Julian combines her acute sense of wonder—like that of a small child—with a passionate faith: in God's presence in all things, in God's faithful care of all creatures. Her three truths are truths indeed for us today as much as for her nearly seven centuries ago.

Now you may like to pick up the small created thing you brought with you. (You can imagine it if you don't have one with you.) Hold it in your hand, look at it, feel its shape and its texture. Think about the passages you have read. Think about God's creation of something so ordinary, so wonderful. And if you can, write down your thoughts in your notebook.

God has gifted all of us with creative talents. Most of these seem insignificant; indeed we may not even recognize that we too have creative gifts. But through their work, the great composers and poets and painters seem to draw us to God who created all beauty and is the source of all inspiration. So it is when we look at moonlight reflected in the sea, or listen to the sound of an instrument skillfully and sensitively played. We are moved to wonder, then to adoration.

> God our Father,
> we thank you for your love.
> God our Maker,
> we thank you for the beauty of the earth.
> We thank you
> We praise you
> We love you
> We adore you.

This is a long chapter. You may choose to take a break here, simply sitting quietly or perhaps going outside for a few moments. You have spent some time meditating on God the Father and Creator; after a short rest you will be asked to think about God the Holy Spirit.

God the Holy Spirit

Come, Holy Spirit, fill the hearts of your faithful and kindle in them the fire of your love.[5]

It is not easy to write about the Holy Spirit of God, not easy to grasp him (or her) with our minds. The Holy Spirit, the third person of the Trinity, is, together with the Father and the Son, God himself. We are able to think of God as a person, in relation to ourselves, *our* Father. We are able to think about God the Son as a person who lived as a human being on earth, in relation to ourselves as brother and friend.

But the Holy Spirit is different, abstract. He can no more be captured by our imagination than he can be confined by time or space or the will of women or men.

Among the symbols of the Holy Spirit are both a flame and a dove; signs with almost contradictory associations. There are many charming medieval paintings of the Annunciation showing Mary and the angel in the foreground. High in one corner is the bearded face of God the Father, and issuing from his mouth are golden rays directed toward Mary. A small dove is winging its way with these rays toward the Virgin. It is the Holy Ghost about to overshadow her so that she will conceive the Son of God in her womb. Such paintings, often very beautiful, have also a certain comic charm to our eyes because of their quaint attempt to encapsulate the Holy Spirit in an acceptable image. Yet we for all our sophistication are no nearer in painting or by any other means to encapsulating, defining, labeling neatly and putting the Holy Spirit in a box than our forebears were. For, after all, the wind "bloweth where it listeth" as the King James Version of the New Testament tells us (John 3:8).

The Holy Spirit has been there since the beginning of time, and is the one who has inspired men and women "from every tribe and nation" with courage and wisdom and the pursuit of goodness. The Spirit has inflamed people from every kind of background with passionate love for God and passionate desire to serve their fellow men and women.

The more we consider and contemplate the persons of the Trinity, the more we become aware of the complex and—it seems to us—paradoxical nature of God. We have seen that God the Father is on the one hand remote and awesome, on the other familiar and accessible. We know that Jesus was born human and divine. The Holy Spirit is even more of a paradox: elusive, uncontainable, free as the air; and yet the one who dwells within us, in the depths of our being. As the Spirit of peace (the dove) and the Spirit of energy (the flame), he is the greatest power for good in our world, and is trapped and frustrated by our lack of cooperation.

Let us try to rid ourselves of too much confusion, and look at what Jesus told his friends about the Holy Spirit, on the night before he died:

"I shall ask the Father,
and he will give you another Advocate
to be with you for ever,
that Spirit of truth
whom the world can never receive
since it neither sees nor knows him;
but you know him,
because he is with you, he is in you."

"I have said these things to you
while still with you;
but the Advocate, the Holy Spirit,
whom the Father will send in my name,
will teach you everything
and remind you of all I have said to you." (John 14:16-17, 25-26)

So Jesus told his disciples that the Holy Spirit would come to be with them. His arrival is dramatic:

When Pentecost day came round, they had all met in one room, when suddenly they heard what sounded like a powerful wind from heaven, the noise of which filled the entire house in which they were sitting; and something appeared to them that seemed like tongues of fire; these separated and came to rest on the head of each of them. They were all filled with the Holy Spirit, and began to speak foreign languages as the Spirit gave them the gift of speech. (Acts 2:1-4)

The effect of the Holy Spirit's coming was even more theatrical. The disciples, who until this moment had been cowed and fearful, were filled with courage and began speaking about Jesus to the crowds. Some people were amazed. They were unable to understand how each person could follow what the disciples were saying in his or her own language. Others accused the disciples of drunkenness.

Then Peter stood up with the Eleven and addressed them in a loud voice:
"Men of Judaea, and all you who live in Jerusalem, make no mistake about this, but listen carefully to what I say. These men are not drunk, as you imagine; why, it is only the third hour of the day. On the contrary, this is what the prophet spoke of:
'In the days to come—it is the Lord who speaks—
I will pour out my spirit on all mankind.
Their sons and daughters shall prophesy,
your young men shall see visions,
your old men shall dream dreams.
Even on my slaves, men and women,
in those days, I will pour out my spirit.
I will display portents in heaven above
and signs on earth below.
The sun will be turned into darkness
and the moon into blood
before the great Day of the Lord dawns.
All who call on the name of the Lord will be saved.' "
(Acts 2:14-21)

Peter's speech reveals the great power of the Holy Spirit. The Spirit can empower us, fill us with the confidence and courage to say and do what we know to be right, and serve as our inspiration when we pray and whenever we meet together in God's name.

The Holy Spirit is also the one who brings out the best in us. If we listen and are guided by the Spirit—instead of listening to and being guided by the popular voice of our materialistic and secular world—we may have the strength to become the people God wants us to be. Then we may bear the fruits Paul writes of in his letter to the Galatians: "What the Spirit brings is . . . love, joy, peace, patience, kindness, goodness, trustfulness, gentleness and self-control" (Gal. 5:22).

It is a daunting thought that this Holy Spirit of God actually lives in us. As Teresa of Avila said,

> Closer is He than breathing:
> Nearer than hands and feet.[6]

Thinking of this we realize how inadequate we are, how feeble our response is, how little we allow the Holy Spirit to bear fruit in us.

The Spirit of God dwells within us, and yet most of the time I, for one, keep him shut away, not allowing his light to shine through me. I am like the young man in the poem by Caryll Houselander:

> If he had only known
> that the God in the picture book,
> is not an old man in the clouds
> but the seed of life in his soul,
> the man would have lived.
> And his life would have flowered
> with the flower of limitless joy.
>
> But he does not know,
> and in him

the Holy Ghost
is a poor little bird
in a cage,
who never sings,
and never opens his wings,
yet never, never
desires to be gone away.[7]

Oh for the courage of the apostle Peter, whose response was so fervent and complete!

Some people are transparent with the light of the Holy Spirit, at least to those with perceptive eyes, like the Native American in this anecdote taken from the writings of Thomas Batty, a Quaker living in the nineteenth century.

I noticed an old Indian in the dining room, of a full and open countenance, wrapped in a buffalo robe, after the wild Indian style, watching me. As that was no new occurrence, however, I thought nothing of it, until he spoke to me by the interpreter. I went to him and he said, "My friend, I can see your heart." This salutation, coming from a wild Comanche, somewhat startled me, particularly as at the time I was much depressed, feeling that there was no good thing there. After a little pause, he continued, "Tell him I see his heart, it good—full of love; he love Indian; I can never hurt man, when I see heart like his—full of love—I love him . . ." I could but believe his heart was touched by a power above his own, and that in him I should find a friend who might be of use to me in the ordering of future events.[8]

Here was the Spirit at work, in an encounter between two strangers.

The Holy Spirit of God is the greatest sign of hope, for us as individuals, especially in our relationships with one another, and for our sad, torn, violence-ridden world.

Now you may like to be in silence, thinking about the Holy Spirit and how he is at work in your life.

SILENCE

There is a very old prayer, which is also a poem, recited in some churches on the feast of Pentecost. It may help your meditation to read it through slowly:

Holy Spirit, Lord of Light
From the clear celestial height
Thy pure beaming radiance give.

Come thou father of the poor,
Come, with treasures which endure;
Come, thou light of all that live!

Thou, of all consolers best,
Thou the soul's delightful guest,
Dost refreshing peace bestow;

Thou in toil art comfort sweet;
Pleasant coolness in the heat;
Solace in the midst of woe.

Light immortal, light divine,
Visit thou these hearts of thine,
And our inmost vision fill:

If thou take thy grace away,
Nothing pure in man will stay;
All his good is turned to ill.

Heal our wounds, our strength renew;
On our dryness pour thy dew;
Wash the stains of guilt away:

Bend the stubborn heart and will;
Melt the frozen, warm the chill;
Guide the steps that go astray.

Thou on us who evermore

Thee confess and thee adore,
With thy sevenfold gifts descend;
Give us comfort when we die;
Give us life with thee on high;
Give us joys which never end.[9]

When you have pondered on your soul's "delightful guest" in quiet for awhile, you may find comfort in the blessing which is given in some churches on Pentecost Sunday:

> This day the Father of light
> has enlightened the minds of the disciples
> by the outpouring of the Holy Spirit.
> May he bless you
> and give you the gifts of the Spirit for ever.
>
> May that fire which hovered over the disciples
> as tongues of flame
> burn out all evil from your hearts
> and make them glow with pure light.
>
> God inspired speech in different tongues
> to proclaim one faith.
> May he strengthen your faith
> and fulfill your hope to see him face to face.
> May Almighty God bless you,
> the Father, and the Son and the Holy Spirit.[10]

By now your mind may be tired. I suggest you get up and stretch and walk over to your window. Open it, feel the fresh air on your face. If it is raining, stretch out your hand and feel the raindrops. Then slowly take in the picture before you. Notice the sky, the ground, anything of nature—birds, trees, grass. Can you see any people? Can you, from your glimpses of them, imagine what their lives might be like?

I open my window. The cool air feels welcome on my face but I soon begin to feel cold and close the window again! It is a rather dull day. It is not raining, but there is no sign of the sun either. I cannot see the sky—the houses opposite are too near and too tall.

In my small garden there are no flowers because this is the dead of winter. I look out at the big round pebbles we collected from the beach one day. I love their shape and their soft colors, gray, pale green, pale rust. There are a few sparrows, such ordinary little birds but somehow always cheerful. Some strangers walk past, a family: mother, father, and two little girls. I smile involuntarily—I am always drawn to children. I see Robert across the street cleaning his windows again. He is quite a young man and he has been unemployed for years. I wonder if he is lonely.

I think of God, who knows when sparrows fall, who made the gray, green, and rust-colored pebbles, who cares for Robert, and for the family who passed by, even if they do not know him.

Can you write a description of what you can see from your window, followed by a reflection on what you have seen?

Lunch

By now you may feel your brain has been working overtime and no doubt used up a good number of calories. You must be hungry and ready for your lunch. Stand and stretch and shake yourself before you sit to enjoy your meal. Here is a grace you may like to say:

> Dear Lord God,
> I think of those of your children
> who are thirsty and hungry today
> while I have so much.
> I ask your blessing on them. Amen.

CHAPTER 4

Early Afternoon

A Letter to God
Reflections on Jesus the Man
Tea

Y ou are now about halfway through the "work" of this day. Some of the things suggested for you to do will take a lot of concentration and energy, and it is important to remember that you should rest or take a break or spend extra time in silence whenever you feel the need. It is likely that you will be tired by the end of the day, but it should be a healthy, peaceful tiredness that you feel. If at any point an exercise you are asked to do seems over-whelming, just "too much," then do not do it. You can leave it completely, or perhaps come back to it later in the day.

A Letter to God

After your lunch, you may like to take a nap, or a walk, or both! When you have wakened or come back, I would like you to sit down and think about writing a letter to God in your notebook. Perhaps you have had a reaction of "shock, horror" to this suggestion. If that is the case, of course you do not have to write the letter, but please do at least think about it, because putting your thoughts down on paper can be a helpful and healthy exercise.

It could be that you hate writing letters anyway, and the thought of writing one to God makes you want to run a mile. Well, like every activity suggested in this book, it is not compulsory. You may choose a compromise—a one-line note to God: "Dear Lord, sometimes I find it hard to believe in you," or "Dear Lord, you know what I'm like!" But if even this is too much, don't worry. Simply omit the exercise and be happy to continue without it.

If you *are* going to do it, write "straight from the heart," telling God how you feel. This will probably not be easy, and may take some time, but it is important that the letter be spontaneous and immediate, not contrived. There is no need to worry about grammar or spelling. No one else need ever see this letter. Write to God as though you were talking to your friend.

The letter may be of use to you later on. Take a few moments' break before moving on to think about Jesus.

Reflections on Jesus the Man

"Mary, do not be afraid; you have won God's favor. Listen! You are to conceive and bear a son, and you must name him Jesus." (Luke 1:30*b*-31)

Jesus Christ, the longed-for savior, lived and died in Palestine two thousand years ago. He was the Son of God and he was also a human being; a man without sin who lived among ordinary people, feeling as they felt, suffering as they suffered, enjoying life as they did. When he was thirty-three years old he died a cruel and shameful death, but three days later he rose to life again and lives with us still through his Spirit. His birth, and the meaning of his life, were foretold by the prophet Isaiah:

The people that walked in darkness
have seen a great light;
on those who live in a land of deep shadow
a light has shone.
You have made their gladness greater,
you have made their joy increase . . .
For there is a child born for us,
a son given to us
and dominion is laid on his shoulders;
and this is the name they give him:
Wonder-Counsellor, Mighty-God,
Eternal-Father, Prince-of-Peace.
Wide is his dominion
in a peace that has no end,
for the throne of David
and for his royal power,
which he establishes and makes secure
in justice and integrity. (Isa. 9:1-2, 5-7)

And sometime after Jesus' death, the apostle Paul wrote of him:

His state was divine,
yet he did not cling
to his equality with God
but emptied himself
to assume the condition of a slave,
and became as men are;
and being as all men are,
he was humbler yet,
even to accepting death,
death on a cross.
But God raised him high
and gave him the name
which is above all other names
so that all beings
in the heavens, on earth and in the underworld,
should bend the knee at the name of Jesus
and that every tongue should acclaim

Jesus Christ as Lord,
to the glory of God the Father. (Phil. 2:6-11)

SILENCE

We know a good deal about God the Son. The story of his life is an inexhaustible source of reflection. Moreover, Jesus is the one who was like us in all things but without sin, the one who knows what it is like to be human.

The twelve apostles were the people who knew him best. They saw him when he was happy, sad, tired, relaxed, angry, laughing, moved with compassion. What was it like actually to live with Jesus, to walk and talk and eat and pray with him every day? In John's Gospel we read of two people who were curious to find out:

> On the following day as John [the Baptist] stood there again with two of his disciples, Jesus passed, and John stared hard at him and said, "Look, there is the lamb of God." Hearing this, the two disciples followed Jesus. Jesus turned around, saw them following and said, "What do you want?" They answered, "Rabbi,"—which means Teacher—"where do you live?" "Come and see" he replied; so they went and saw where he lived, and stayed with him the rest of that day. (John 1:35-39)

"Come and see," said Jesus.

Suppose he said that to you? I am going to ask you to think about this. Think about it prayerfully. What would it be like to spend a day with Jesus? Let your imagination run free, and then describe your day in your notebook. Once, on a Quiet Day, a group of us were asked to do this. Here is what one person wrote:

A Day with Jesus

Jesus took my hand. He said, "Let's go through the cornfields—that way we may not bump into any of the scribes and Pharisees!"

72

I felt very happy, light-hearted even. The sun was shining and there were wildflowers at the edge of the fields. We laughed and joked a little. Then suddenly a little boy was running toward us. He came up to Jesus panting, and took hold of his robe.

"Please come," he said. "It's my mother. She's very ill; they think she is going to die. Oh, I'm so afraid!"

Jesus did not hurry but he smiled down at the little boy and the anxiety went out of the child's eyes. We continued to walk toward the village. Jesus was holding the boy's hand now, instead of mine, but I did not mind. I was sure of his love for me and because of him I loved the boy too; I loved everyone we might meet that day.

All the same, it was a bit of a shock when we reached the village. It was full of people, and some of them were terribly disabled. Many of them were dirty, and the smell was horrible. There was a lot of wailing and groaning, and people pushing one another to get to where they thought Jesus would come. When they saw him there was a sudden hush. Then people began to call his name, and shove one another out of the way quite ruthlessly. Jesus remained calm. First, he went with the boy to his house, and—it seemed only a few moments later—came out again with a young woman looking the picture of health.

"Thank you, thank you!" she was saying. "I can't ever thank you enough. I thought I was going to die!"

Jesus only smiled and ruffled the boy's hair before he began to walk among the crowd, blessing the people and healing them.

For awhile I just stood and stared. Then I moved away. I went into a field and sat down on top of a rock, watching everything that happened. After awhile I began to feel exhausted. I was doing nothing, but Jesus was working without ceasing, listening carefully to each person, touching them, even the lepers, even the very dirty ones. I was tired out, just watching.

I must have fallen asleep, because when I woke up everything was quiet. I looked up to see Jesus standing over me, still smiling.

"Come and eat," he said.

I sat up and looked around. The sun was low in the sky and the crowd had vanished. A few people were sitting around a fire in the next field. Then I saw the young woman, the boy's mother, carrying something out to them. The smell caught my nostrils.

"Come on," said Jesus, pulling me to my feet. "I'm hungry. Aren't you? Jacob's father has invited us to celebrate his wife's recovery."

We sat around the fire, eating and drinking and joking and telling stories. I had never met any of Jesus' friends before, but I felt I belonged with them. Then suddenly a kind of panic gripped me. He wasn't there.

"Where is he?" I asked the man sitting next to me. He grinned.

"Don't worry," he said. "He's just gone off to pray. He often does that."

I wished I could go with him. I got to my feet. But Jacob's mother said gently, "Don't go after him. He likes to be alone." So I stayed where I was, and sure enough, just as it was beginning to grow dark, he came back.

"I'm afraid there aren't any beds for us, Anna," he said. "Can you sleep in the open?"

"Yes, of course," I said. I thought I could do anything as long as he was there.

Someone found me a blanket, and there was a grassy mound for a pillow. I lay there, looking up at the brilliant stars and thinking, "This is wonderful!"

I must have fallen asleep almost immediately, but I woke up in the middle of the night. I could hear a wolf howling in the distance and I was shivering with cold. All at once, Jesus was there. He was bending over me, gently covering me with a sheepskin. He said, "Anna, do not be afraid."

SILENCE

Try to write a description of your own imagined day with Jesus. Your day might be completely different. You might like to think how it would be if he was accompanying you on an ordinary working day.

Here are some passages from the Gospels that tell us something about Jesus. They reveal his humanity, showing how he felt about things and giving us an inkling as to what sort of person he was. In Victorian times and earlier, Jesus became sentimentalized and so we have hymns and carols that include lines like: "Gentle Jesus, meek and mild"[1] and "Christian children all must be mild, obedient, good as he."[2] But we realize now that Jesus was a forthright young man; compassionate certainly, but capable of toughness when it was necessary.

> Now one sabbath he happened to be taking a walk through the cornfields, and his disciples were picking ears of corn, rubbing them in their hands and eating them. Some of the Pharisees said, "Why are you doing something that is forbidden on the sabbath day?" Jesus answered them, "So you have not read what David did when he and his followers were hungry—how he went into the house of God, took the loaves of offering and ate them and gave them to his followers, loaves which only the priests are allowed to eat?" And he said to them, "The Son of Man is master of the sabbath." (Luke 6:1-5)

You may like to spend a few moments now imagining yourself taking a stroll through the fields with Jesus.

I particularly like this passage because it is unusual, giving us a glimpse of Jesus enjoying some relaxation—not teaching, not healing, not praying, but simply taking a walk through the fields with his friends on a Saturday morning.

The Gospels were written to teach us about the ministry of Jesus, and so they are almost exclusively taken up with the serious business of his life: his teaching and his healing, until we come to his passion, death, and resurrection. There is not much room for trivia, nor perhaps would the reader be expected to be interested in them.

Yet, fortunately, the setting for this story does make it plain that there was, however occasionally, some time for leisure in the life of Jesus and that once at least he chose to spend it in this way. Jesus was not ordinary, but he was "normal"; not an austere monk, not a workaholic, not a person who set himself apart from the doings of other folk.

What do you imagine they were talking about? The weather? Sports? Politics? War? Peter: about his wife or children perhaps? Jesus: about his mother? Perhaps they were singing hymns or the popular songs of their day. Who would be walking closest to Jesus? Would they change places? You could write your ideas in your notebook.

But of course the purpose of Luke's narrative is not to tell us this. Rather it is to illustrate an important aspect of the teaching of Jesus. The Pharisees are pleased to catch him, or at any rate some of his disciples, in the wrong, and are quick to challenge him. The challenge is pretty feeble: all the disciples are guilty of is eating ears of corn as they walked through the fields on the Sabbath.

Jesus is never afraid to encounter such critics or to meet their challenges. In all his clashes with the authorities he remains calm. Often he is quick-witted, and until the last hours of his life, he invariably comes out on top.

"The Son of Man is master of the sabbath," he says. But this teaching is not simply about observance of the Sabbath, it goes deeper than that. Jesus was distressed and angered by the complacency and hypocrisy of the Pharisees. He saw so clearly that they were repressing themselves and the people by their insistence on the importance of petty rules, to such an extent that obedience to the law took precedence over freedom and love. Jesus spoke out against this, sometimes vehemently:

> "Alas for you, scribes and Pharisees, you hypocrites! You who shut up the kingdom of heaven in men's faces, neither going in yourselves nor allowing others to go in who want to." (Matt. 23:13)

and again,

> "Alas for you, scribes and Pharisees, you hypocrites! You
> who are like whitewashed tombs that look handsome on
> the outside, but inside are full of dead men's bones and
> every kind of corruption. In the same way you appear to
> people from the outside like good honest men, but inside
> you are full of hypocrisy and lawlessness." (Matt. 23:27-28)

Sadly, the things that Jesus hated and fought to change in
his day have crept into the church that exists in his name.
In so many of our traditions we restrict and repress people
by rules and laws and hierarchies, getting further and
further away from the simplicity and openness of Jesus.

We need laws, in our churches as well as in society.
What we do not need are the sort of laws that inhibit us
from living and loving to the full.

I know, for instance, that many Roman Catholics question the rule that makes it obligatory for them to attend
Mass on a Sunday. People of other denominations, whose
congregations are dwindling, may feel a certain envy when
they see the Catholic church in their neighborhood over-
flowing not once but two or three times on a Sunday. But
we have to ask: does God want people to worship out of
obedience to a law, or out of love? Yet discipline is undoubtedly of great value, and many people are attracted to
the Roman Catholic church precisely because it is so
authoritarian and structured.

Equally we have gone astray in the kind of false importance we attach to the leaders of some of our churches,
according them a lifestyle that is hardly in keeping with
that of Jesus himself. It happened in his own day:

> Addressing the people and his disciples Jesus said, "The
> scribes and Pharisees occupy the chair of Moses. You must
> therefore do what they tell you and listen to what they say;
> but do not be guided by what they do: since they do not
> practice what they preach. They tie up heavy burdens and

lay them on men's shoulders, but will they lift a finger to move them? Not they! Everything they do is done to attract attention, like wearing broader phylacteries and longer tassels, like wanting to take the place of honor at banquets and the front seats in the synagogues, being greeted obsequiously in the market squares and having people call them Rabbi." (Matt. 23:1-7)

The Quakers and Free Churches have done well to get away from the pomp and grandeur that still captivate the older traditions in the Christian churches.

Sometimes I have been present at a service led by a bishop, a man I believe to be humble, compassionate, and full of integrity: in a word, Christlike. But the ceremony demands that he stand in the sanctuary, dressed in a gown of glittering gold, and my guess is that for him, as for me, this feels like a sign of contradiction. For Jesus was humble, he was the servant, he lived in simplicity.

But there is another way of looking at these things. I remember once being shocked when a missionary friend of mine told me of a magnificent new cathedral that had been built in a small African country where most of the people were extremely poor. But when I told him how I felt he said, "I understand your reaction. But the people themselves are delighted with the cathedral. For them it is a fitting tribute to the glory of God, and they are happy to have something concrete to blaze forth their love for him."

The Pharisees angered Jesus because of their obsession with the law, their preoccupation with their own importance, and most of all with their indifference to the welfare of the people.

SILENCE

[Jesus] said to them, "You must come away to some lonely place all by yourselves and rest for a while"; for there were so many coming and going that the apostles had no time even to eat. So they went off in a boat to a lonely place where they could be by themselves. But people saw them going, and many could guess where; and from every town they all hurried to the place on foot and reached it before them. So as he stepped ashore he saw a large crowd; and he took pity on them because they were like sheep without a shepherd, and he set himself to teach them at some length. (Mark 6:31-34)

I was first struck by this passage after an experience of my own. At one time I taught in a school for disabled children. Any kind of teaching, undertaken conscientiously, is hard work, and any kind of work with people with special needs is heavily demanding. I do not complain about this; my job in that school was rewarding and I learned a great deal from it. But I did get tired.

One day I happened to be particularly exhausted. I was longing to get home, and when the bell rang at four o'clock I hurriedly packed my bags and strode across the hall to the main entrance, looking neither to the left nor the right.

I heard a voice calling my name. I hesitated, half turned and saw it was a fourteen-year-old child from my class. Like most disabled teenagers, she had serious worries about sex and love. She had confided in me several times and I had said to her, "Any time you want to talk, don't hesitate to ask." So she asked, and I said, "I'm sorry, Jenny. I've got to get home. Another time . . . ?" And I left her.

Shortly afterward I read this passage from Mark. I felt an enormous surge of sympathy for Jesus, tired-out Jesus, when he was faced with an eager crowd. I also felt shame that I had not responded to my student as he did to people he met.

But I am not like Jesus, at least only a little like him. I am not capable of that depth of compassion and self-sacrifice. I wish I were, and I am full of admiration for those people, Christians or unbelievers, who not only give up their comfort but risk their lives for others. I have just been reading about some Roman Catholic nuns, the Medical Missionaries of Mary, who work in a hospital in Kotovi, in the province of Masaka, southern Uganda. Masaka is one of the regions in Uganda most affected by the AIDS epidemic, and the sisters are struggling from day to day with the human suffering caused by it. Like everyone else, I have seen pictures on television of young nurses in Somalia and young aid workers in Bosnia who have given up everything to serve others.

For ordinary folk like me, it is difficult to know where to draw the line between allowing ourselves to become exhausted, overstressed, and burned out, and being generous with our time, energy, and attention.

Jesus was untroubled by the need to draw such lines; he did not complain that he was suffering from compassion fatigue. He saw the need and got on with the job.

Please spend some time now, reflecting on this incident in the life of Jesus.

SILENCE

He was setting out on a journey when a man ran up, knelt before him and put this question to him, "Good master, what must I do to inherit eternal life?" Jesus said to him, "Why do you call me good? No one is good but God alone. You know the commandments: You must not kill; You must not commit adultery; You must not steal; You must not bring false witness; You must not defraud; Honor your father and mother." And he said to him, "Master, I have kept all these from my earliest days." Jesus looked steadily at him and loved him, and he said, "There is one thing you lack. Go and sell everything you own and give the money to the poor, and you will have treasure in heaven; then come, follow me." But his face fell at these words and he went away sad, for he was a man of great wealth. (Mark 10:17-22)

When we read Gospel incidents of the life of Jesus, we can discover different levels of meaning. On the surface, the lesson of this story is that following Christ is costly.

The young man was full of goodness and eagerness to follow Jesus, but he could not give up his money and his possessions—at least as far as we know. He went away sad. Did he later find the courage and generosity to let go of his wealth and give his whole heart to Jesus?

The Gospels are not like a story with a beginning, a middle, and an end. Often they are just fragments of narrative that leave us guessing and wondering what happened next. This may be untidy, but it allows us to give free rein to our imaginations. And what is more interesting, the Gospel stories speak to different people at different times in different ways. God speaks to us through Scripture, but he does not necessarily say the same thing to you as he does to me.

For this reason, it is very important for you to keep a time for your own silent reflection on these passages. Your thoughts are of much greater value than my words.

In the passage you have just read, the teaching was about the danger of riches, or perhaps the idolizing of riches. But for me the story is not only about wealth. It seems to be about letting go and the freedom that comes from letting go. The young man clung to his money and could not imagine coping without it. We all cling tight to all sorts of things: our own reputation, the image we present to others, our security, our comfort, our circle of "nice" friends, our ambition, our success, our position in society, in the church, or in our workplace—and because we hold fast to these things, afraid to let go, we are not free to become single-hearted in our response to God.

These are my thoughts when I read the account of the meeting of Jesus and the rich young man. What I *feel* is something different. I feel moved to sadness by the story, sadness not so much for the young man as for Jesus himself. Mark tells us that when Jesus saw this young man he looked at him steadily and loved him. Obviously Jesus loved everyone who came his way, because that was the essence of him, to love. But it is not often that the Gospels mention his specific love for another person. We know that Jesus loved his friend Lazarus, because when he wept at the tomb of Lazarus the bystanders said, "See how much he loved him!" (John 11:36). John tells us of "the disciple Jesus loved" (John 13:23), apparently meaning himself. When he saw the rich young man Jesus was drawn to him and must have hoped very much that he would join his band of followers. On a human level, when the young man walked away, Jesus must have felt rejected.

Because of the special relationship he seems to have had with John and with the other young man, it has been suggested that Jesus was a homosexual, but there is no evidence to support this. The Greek word for love, referring to the love of Jesus for John, is the same word as is used to describe God's love for us. Again, the same word is used for Jesus' feelings for the rich young man, and in the celebrated passage about love in chapter thirteen of Paul's first letter to the Corinthians. As far as this word *agape* can be exactly translated, it means brotherly or sisterly love. We are also told: "Jesus loved Martha and her sister and Lazarus" (John 11:5). The Greeks were more subtle than we are in their use of the word *love*, and had a completely different word (*eros*) to indicate sexual love.

There are also presentations like the film *Jesus Christ Superstar* that imply that there was a sexual relationship between Mary Magdalene and Jesus. There are no authentic grounds for this, unless an eye to the box office counts as authentic!

We know absolutely nothing about the sexuality of Jesus, but since he was fully human it seems safe to assume that he was not asexual.

The rich young man went away. Rejection in all its forms is very hard to bear. I remember to this day how I felt when I was not chosen to be a prefect in my school (prefects were elected by popular vote), and how I felt when my fiancé told me he loved someone else—but of course there are far worse rejections. The natural mother of our adopted son decided, as soon as she knew she had conceived, that she did not want him; she gave him up for adoption just after he was born. He was twice fostered and twice rejected and by the time he was three he had given up expecting to be loved.

In one sense it seems absurd to feel pity for Jesus because a young man he had known only for a few moments walked away instead of following him. After all, Jesus was a man of authority and strength, loved and admired by hundreds of people. It is hardly my place to pity the Son of God! And yet, I do. I suppose it is precisely because we know him to be divine that Jesus seems so vulnerable in his humanity. We are drawn to love him, and part of loving anyone is suffering when they suffer, feeling their pain even when it is nothing more than a pinprick.

My reflections on this passage are personal to me. You may think and feel very differently as you pause now to ponder on the story in silence.

SILENCE

Of the four passages in this section that I have chosen so that you can reflect on the humanity of Jesus, the last one is probably the most familiar. This is because most of us have read and heard, perhaps every year in Holy Week or on Good Friday, the story of the passion of our Lord Jesus Christ, beginning with the Last Supper and ending with the Crucifixion. Those who are accustomed to praying the rosary will have meditated often on Jesus' agony in the garden of Gethsemane.

He then left to make his way as usual to the Mount of Olives, with the disciples following. When they reached the place he said to them, "Pray not to be put to the test." Then he withdrew from them, about a stone's throw away, and knelt down and prayed. "Father," he said, "if you are willing, take this cup away from me. Nevertheless, let your will be done, not mine." Then an angel appeared to him, coming from heaven to give him strength. In his anguish he prayed even more earnestly, and his sweat fell to the ground like great drops of blood. (Luke 22:39-44)

This is a deeply moving account, and one that shows Jesus seemingly stripped for awhile of his divinity. He is quite simply a terrified man. The thought of the ordeal before him was overwhelming. In his fear and panic he turns to his Father, but he does not receive the answer he longs for. God does not say, "All right, you don't have to go through with it."

The Son of God was destined to die on the cross for the redemption of humankind. Jesus the man did not want to do this. His whole being shrank from the task.

It is arguable that we are most moved to worship Jesus, not when he does marvelous things because he is God, but when he is seen in all his frailty, and especially here when with a supreme effort he overcomes his weakness and accepts the will of his Father.

Some of us in times of great anguish have cried to God for a comforting answer and found none. I remember that when our little son was dying we prayed so fervently that he would be saved; he died. Jesus prayed long and earnestly for the cup to be taken away, but it was not. He had to drink it. He is indeed our brother and our friend. In his humanity he shares our pain and bewilderment.

Please pray for awhile in silence as you reflect on the agony of Jesus.

SILENCE

Remember your own times of agony. It may help to write them down. Caryll Houselander wrote a poem that vividly describes the humanity of Jesus:

> God abides in men
> Because Christ has put on
> the nature of man, like a garment,
> and worn it to his own shape.
> He has put on everyone's life.
> He has fitted himself to the little child's dress,
> to the shepherd's coat of sheepskin,
> to the workman's coat
> to the king's red robes,
> to the snowy loveliness of the wedding garment,
> and to the drab
> and the sad, simple battle-dress.
>
> Christ has put on man's nature, and given him back his
>   humanness
> worn to the shape
> of limitless love, and warm from the touch
> of his life.[3]

SILENCE

Tea

You will probably need a break now, after this silence. You man like to have a cup of tea and a biscuit, if you are hungry, and perhaps go outside for a little while.

CHAPTER 5

Late Afternoon

Reflections on Jesus,
the Son of God
Break

This chapter, like the last one, looks at Jesus. You may be flagging a little by now and not feel like concentrating too hard. In John's Gospel Jesus makes several statements about himself. I have included five of these, with the passages that follow, and made some reflections on each of them. They are:

- I am the bread of life.
- I am the light of the world.
- I am the gate of the sheepfold.
- I am the good shepherd.
- I am the true vine.

I would like to suggest that you first read through the Gospel passages on their own, and then decide which you would like to use for reflection. It may be all of them; it may be just one—whatever feels right for you.

I have made my own reflections on each passage, but your own thoughts will be of much more value, and it may help you to jot some of them down in your notebook.

The Spirit of the Lord is upon me, because he hath anointed me to preach the gospel to the poor; he hath sent me to heal the brokenhearted, to preach deliverance to the captives, and recovering of sight to the blind, to set at liberty them that are bruised. (Luke 4:18 KJV)

Jesus chose this text from Isaiah (61:1-2) to read to the people of Nazareth in their synagogue, and when he had finished he said, "This text is being fulfilled today even as you listen" (Luke 4:21). It was a description of his own ministry.

Jesus, the Son of God, submitted to crucifixion so that we might be saved. He was sent to live in the world for this purpose. He died at the age of thirty-three, and the last three years of his life were spent in the service of others. He was sent to preach, to heal, to serve, and to set free.

Are you among the poor, the bruised, the brokenhearted? If not, do you know anyone who is? Do you long to be set free? Do you feel the need for Jesus? You may like to think about these things for a few moments.

SILENCE

Reflections on Jesus, the Son of God

In the last chapter we saw evidence of the humanity of Jesus. Now I ask you to look at him from a rather different standpoint.

Studying and reflecting on some of the statements Jesus makes about himself can help us to understand a little more about the Son of God.

"I am the bread of life.
He who comes to me will never be hungry." (John 6:35)

Bread is what we call "the staff of life," the basic food without which we cannot live. In Mexico the staple food is beans, in India, rice, in Ireland it used to be the potato—but Jesus is using bread as a symbol of essential nourishment for everyone. We need bread for our bodies to stay alive and well. We need Jesus for our souls to stay alive and well. Without the Spirit of Jesus, we can only exist, we cannot live. He said, "It is the Spirit that gives life" (John 6:63), and the writer of Psalm 104 cries to God: "You take back your Spirit, they die" (Ps. 104:29). I believe in this truth, but the words "He who comes to me will never be hungry" make me think of those who are starving in the poor countries of our world.

They are undoubtedly hungry with a hunger that few of us in the north and west will ever know, a hunger that gnaws at their vitals and leads to a slow, miserable death, especially agonizing for parents who have to watch their children die in this way. Before they can be hungry for Jesus, the bread of life, their bodies must be fed.

Jesus spoke the words "I am the bread of life" about himself before his arrest. And at supper the night before he died, he took bread and broke it and shared it among his friends, saying, "This is my body given for you; do this in remembrance of me" (Luke 22:20 NJB). When we receive bread in Holy Communion, we are receiving Jesus, the bread of life, who comes to nourish our souls, who longs to make us "other Christs."

Here are some questions:

- Can you live without food?
- Do you ever fast?
- Can you live without Jesus, the bread of life?
- Is there anything you can do for the starving?
- Is there anything you can do for those who do not perceive themselves as hungry for Jesus?

You could write your responses and then spend some time thinking about the meaning of Jesus' words.

SILENCE

88

"I am the light of the world. Whoever follows me will never walk in darkness but will have the light of life." (John 8:12 NRSV)

Light is a symbol of goodness, and darkness a symbol of evil. Our earth is lit by the sun. At sunrise the darkness is dispelled. Like Jesus, the sun brings warmth and brightness into our lives. As flowers open and fruit ripens in the sun, so in being receptive to the outpouring of the Spirit of Jesus we can grow in wisdom and holiness.

Isaiah foretold the birth of Jesus, saying:

> The people that walked in darkness
> have seen a great light;
> on those who live in a land of deep shadow
> a light has shone. (Isa. 9:1)

And in Psalm 27:1 we read:

> The Lord is my light and my help;
> whom shall I fear?

Here are some more questions:

- What do you think Jesus meant when he said, "I am the light of the world"?
- Do you know any people who walk in darkness or live in a land of deep shadow?

I think I know people who walk in darkness.

They are some of those who are HIV positive, or suffering from AIDS, the people who know they must soon die and are afraid, the ones who live in fear and secrecy and shame.

They are the people locked away in prison who should never have been put there; the innocent, the prisoners of conscience, the victims of others' devious cruelty, those who have little or no control over their actions.

And they are the people who suffer from real, deep depression, the ones who can see no light anywhere, and feel no hope.

We know that Jesus also said, "*You* are the light of the world" (Matt. 5:14 my italics). How can we respond to this?

SILENCE

> So Jesus spoke to them again:
> "I tell you most solemnly,
> I am the gate of the sheepfold.
> All others who have come
> are thieves and brigands;
> but the sheep took no notice of them.
> I am the gate.
> Anyone who enters through me will be safe:
> he will go freely in and out
> and be sure of finding pasture.
> The thief comes
> only to steal and kill and destroy.
> I have come
> so that they may have life
> and have it to the full." (John 10:7-10)

I begin by concentrating on the end of this extract because it happens to be one of my favorite pieces of Scripture. It disproves any theory that Jesus wants us to live narrow, rigid, puritanical lives. Not only does he want us to live our lives to the full, but he actually came on earth that we might do so.

What does living life to the full mean for you? For me it means not staying always in my own cozy world, but going out to meet others from all kinds of different backgrounds, with all sorts of different personalities, and sharing their lives for awhile. It means listening to music, looking at paintings, reading poetry, enjoying the beauty of nature. It means working hard and having fun. It means praying. It means seizing life with both hands.

For you, it may mean different things, according to your circumstances. You may like to record them in your notebook.

Jesus says that he is the gate of the sheepfold. Elsewhere he says, "I am the way." Does this mean that we can only come to salvation, to heaven, to the kingdom of God through Jesus? I think the answer must be "Yes and No." I am certain that we do not have to be Christians to enter the kingdom of heaven. But we need to have been touched, in his mysterious way, by the Spirit of Jesus, and this can happen even to those who have never heard his name.

Jesus speaks the reassuring words:

> "Anyone who enters through me will be safe:
> he will go freely in and out
> and be sure of finding pasture." (John 10:9)

We are promised, in the same breath, security and freedom. We can trust our God to hold us, and to go on holding us, in his everlasting love. But at the same time he trusts us: we are free to explore and experience life. It is like the delicate balance a parent tries to keep between sheltering his or her children from danger and giving them opportunities to learn and to grow.

Now you can give yourself time to think about all these things, and to thank God for his wisdom and his care for you.

SILENCE

The next passage is a continuation of the last one.

"I am the good shepherd:
the good shepherd is one who lays down his life for his
   sheep.

91

The hired man, since he is not the shepherd
and the sheep do not belong to him,
abandons the sheep and runs away
as soon as he sees a wolf coming,
and then the wolf attacks and scatters the sheep;
this is because he is only a hired man
and has no concern for the sheep.
I am the good shepherd;
I know my own
and my own know me,
just as the Father knows me
and I know the Father;
and I lay down my life for my sheep.
And there are other sheep I have
that are not of this fold,
and these I have to lead as well.
They too will listen to my voice,
and there will be only one flock,
and one shepherd.
The Father loves me,
because I lay down my life
in order to take it up again.
No one takes it from me;
I lay it down of my own free will,
and as it is in my power to lay it down,
so it is in my power to take it up again;
and this is the command I have been given by my Father."
(John 10:11-18)

Jesus abruptly changes his metaphor. He has just said, "I am the gate of the sheepfold." Now he is saying, "I am the good shepherd."

It is interesting to look at the characteristics of the good shepherd. First, he is the one who lays down his life for his sheep, just as Jesus would lay down his life for us. Next, he is the one who cares for his sheep and will not abandon them, no matter what. Then comes something more surprising: "And there are other sheep I have that are not of this fold" (John 10:16a). What can this mean? Although the text can be adapted for use in promoting Christian unity, especially the lines "there will be only one flock, and one shepherd," this can hardly be what Jesus had in mind since there were not yet any people calling themselves Christians, let alone any *divided* Christians.

So it seems reasonable to suppose that Jesus' words refer to the "outsiders," the pagans, those of other faiths.

In the last part of this extract from John's Gospel, Jesus is foretelling his death and resurrection.

You may like to look again at the best loved of all the psalms. Jesus must have recited it and reflected on it very often:

> The Lord is my shepherd;
> there is nothing I shall want.
> Fresh and green are the pastures
> where he gives me repose.
> Near restful waters he leads me,
> to revive my drooping spirit.
> He guides me along the right path;
> he is true to his name.
> If I should walk in the valley of darkness
> no evil would I fear.
> You are there with your crook and your staff;
> with these you give me comfort.
>
> You have prepared a banquet for me
> in the sight of my foes.
> My head you have anointed with oil;
> my cup is overflowing.
>
> Surely goodness and kindness shall follow me
> all the days of my life.
> In the Lord's own house shall I dwell
> for ever and ever. (Ps. 23)

Now you can compare the passage from John with Psalm 23.

- How do you feel about being a sheep?
- How do you feel about belonging to the flock of Jesus?

There is a Japanese variation on Psalm 23 that you may find helpful for yourself on this day:

The Lord is my Pace-setter—I shall not rush.
He makes me stop for quiet intervals,
He provides me with images of stillness which restore my
    serenity,
He leads me in ways of efficiency through calmness of
    mind,
And his guidance is Peace.
Even though I have a great many things to accomplish each
    day,
I will not fret, for his presence is here.
His timelessness, his all-importance, will keep me in
    balance.
He prepares refreshment and renewal in the midst of my
    activity
By anointing my mind with his oils of tranquility
My cup of joyous energy overflows.
Truly harmony and effectiveness shall be the fruits of my
    hours
For I shall walk in the Pace of my Lord
And dwell in his house for ever.[1]

Now you may like to pause for a "quiet interval."

SILENCE

"I am the true vine,
and my Father is the vinedresser.
Every branch in me that bears no fruit
he cuts away,
and every branch that does bear fruit he prunes
to make it bear even more.
You are pruned already,

by means of the word that I have spoken to you.
Make your home in me, as I make mine in you.
As a branch cannot bear fruit all by itself,
but must remain part of the vine,
neither can you unless you remain in me.
I am the vine,
you are the branches.
Whoever remains in me, with me in him,
bears fruit in plenty;
for cut off from me you can do nothing." (John 15:1-5)

Here is a new image: the vine.

Again, as with the sheep, we have the notion of belonging, of closeness: "I am the vine, you are the branches" (John 15:5*a*). Jesus wants his followers to bear fruit. Fruitfulness was very important to him. We see his uncharacteristic vehemence when he addresses the barren fig tree, saying, "May no one ever eat fruit from you again" (Mark 11:14). He was angry because there was no fruit on the tree. And in the parable of the talents the man who simply buried his talent in the ground found no leniency:

"Last came forward the man who had the one talent. 'Sir,' said he 'I had heard you were a hard man, reaping where you have not sown and gathering where you have not scattered; so I was afraid, and I went off and hid your talent in the ground. Here it is; it was yours, you have it back.' But his master answered him, 'You wicked and lazy servant! So you knew that I reap where I have not sown and gather where I have not scattered? Well then, you should have deposited my money with the bankers, and on my return I would have recovered my capital with interest. So now, take the talent from him and give it to the man who has the five talents.'" (Matt. 25:24-28)

But what does this mean for us, to bear fruit? Perhaps it means that we should not keep our gifts hidden, but have the courage to use whatever gifts we may have. In other words, if you can sing, sing!

I think it also means that we should not lead sterile, static lives. To bear fruit we do not need to produce anything concrete, to "achieve," to be successful in worldly terms, nor do we necessarily have to be active. A life of prayer can bear fruit in abundance. Contemplative orders of monks and nuns bear witness to this, as do individuals, housebound for one reason or another, who devote a large part of their waking hours to prayer.

What all of us need is to be receptive to the action of the Holy Spirit, so that we may grow in holiness and love. And as we have seen already, the fruits of the Spirit are: "love, joy, peace, patience, kindness, goodness, trustfulness, gentleness and self-control" (Gal. 5:22).

Think about the fruitfulness of your own life, and perhaps record your thoughts in your notebook.

There is one line in the passage about the vine that speaks to me more than any other: "Make your home in me, as I make mine in you." Here is a mystery, but nevertheless one that I find consoling. How can we live in Christ, and he in us? In another place in the same Gospel, Jesus makes this promise:

> "If anyone loves me he will keep my word,
> and my Father will love him,
> and we shall come to him
> and make our home with him." (John 14:23)

I find this a staggering concept, awe-inspiring, humbling, comforting, and challenging, that my God should come to dwell in me!

What effect does this thought have on you?

SILENCE

I think that when Jesus uses metaphors to describe himself—the bread of life, the light of the world, the gate of the sheepfold, the good shepherd, and the true vine, and indeed when we read all of the words of his last discourse before his crucifixion—we are very much aware that he is the Son of God. He speaks with divine authority and assurance.

Yet sometimes it seems as though Jesus himself was more keenly aware of his divinity, and at other times of his humanity. If we look at the story of Lazarus, we see that when Jesus received the message that Lazarus was ill, his reaction was divinely confident. He said, "The sickness will end not in death but in God's glory" (John 11:4). John goes on to say: "Jesus loved Martha and her sister and Lazarus, yet when he heard that Lazarus was ill he stayed where he was for two more days" (John 11:5-6). Jesus, as God, is certain that all will be well.

Then he journeys to Judea, and finds that Lazarus has been dead for four days. Martha confronts Jesus, saying, "If you had been here, my brother would not have died" (John 11:21). Jesus answers her with supreme confidence, telling her that her brother will rise again. And when Martha says, "I know he will rise again at the resurrection on the last day," Jesus replies:

"I am the resurrection.
If anyone believes in me, even though he dies he will live,
and whoever lives and believes in me will never die."
(John 11:25-26)

But then, something happens. The whole tenor of the story changes. Jesus becomes wholly vulnerable, manifestly human.

Mary went to Jesus, and as soon as she saw him she threw herself at his feet, saying, "Lord, if you had been here, my brother would not have died." At the sight of her tears and those of the Jews who followed her, Jesus said in great distress, with a sigh that came straight from the heart,

"Where have you put him?" They said, "Lord, come and see." Jesus wept; and the Jews said, "See how much he loved him!" (John 11:32-36)

Perhaps you could read through chapter 11 of John's Gospel as far as verse 44, pondering on Jesus the divine and Jesus the human.

> The Lord comes into our world
> And he comes most of all for the poor
> He brings light into their darkness
> And hope in their despairing.
> He brings love to those who have never known loving
> And bandages the wounds of all who are hurt.
> In his birth and his living
> In his loving and his dying,
> He gives us, his broken ones,
> His peace and his healing;
> He gives us himself.[2]

SILENCE

You have been thinking about Jesus in the last two sessions, and before that you were reflecting on God the Father and God the Holy Spirit. You may like to finish this chapter by saying the wonderful prayer of the apostle Paul, which in its thinking encompasses all three persons of God's holy Trinity. You can make the prayer your own by substituting "me" for "you" and so on.

> This, then, is what I pray, kneeling before the Father, from whom every family, whether spiritual or natural, takes its name:
> Out of his infinite glory, may he give you the power through his Spirit for your hidden self to grow strong, so that Christ may live in your hearts through faith, and then, planted in love and built on love, you will with all the saints have strength to grasp the breadth and the length, the height and the depth; until, knowing the love of Christ,

which is beyond all knowledge, you are filled with the utter fullness of God.

Glory be to him whose power, working in us, can do infinitely more than we can ask or imagine; glory be to him from generation to generation in the Church and in Christ Jesus for ever and ever. Amen. (Eph. 3:14-21)

Could you write in your notebook a prayer to Jesus as you have discovered him to be through your reflection, and then draw the bread, the gate, the light, the vine—whatever symbol of Jesus seems appropriate for you?

Break

You probably deserve another cup of tea, or depending on how much work you have done on chapter 5, or how tired you are, you may like to take a proper break now and have your supper. There is bound to be considerable variation here: it will depend on how long you have spent in silence, what time you are used to eating, and whether you are hungry or gasping for fresh air. The next chapter is quite demanding, but the last one is comparatively short. Do whatever suits you at this moment.

SILENCE

CHAPTER 6

Evening

Reflections on Yourself
Supper

Know thyself.[1]

For several hours today you have been concentrating on thoughts of God. Now I am going to ask you to think instead for awhile about yourself. In fact, this is not such an about-turn as it may at first seem, because it is inevitable that when we reflect on God's majesty, glory, purity, faithfulness, and love, we cannot help but become aware of our own littleness, emptiness, and inadequacy. The more brightly the sun shines on the door of my house, the more clearly I can see the cracks, the fading paintwork, the rusting door knocker, the tiny flaws and blotches in the woodwork.

You may feel the last thing you want to do is look at yourself. But, as it happens, self-knowledge is a necessary step on the path to holiness and wholeness.

In the fourteenth century, an English mystic, about whom we know nothing—not even his name—except what we can glean from his writings, wrote *The Cloud of Unknowing.* This is a little book of profound spirituality, in which the writer is teaching his young friend the art of contemplation. He writes robustly, not pussyfooting around in the fear of offending the sensitivity of his pupil.

Very near the beginning of the book, he says, "Pause for a moment, you wretched weakling, and take stock of yourself. Who are you, and what have you deserved, to be called like this by our Lord?"[2] A little later in the book he exhorts his pupil further: "Strain every nerve in every possible way to know and experience yourself as you really are."

So I urge you, too, to take stock of yourself. I do not mean to encourage morbid introspection, but a healthy, honest examination of the sort of person you are.

It is not an easy task. As we grow older we realize that it is impossible to know even one person thoroughly. We are such complex creatures, and all the buffetings and stresses that life deals us lead us to construct a sort of defense around ourselves, to black out all the windows so that no one can see inside. Most of the time we do this quite unconsciously. It is not that we particularly wish to be secretive or deceitful, but as we struggle for survival and success and try to evade all those things that produce fear in us, we construct layer upon layer of protective skins over the deepest reality of ourselves.

It is true that a good friend is someone with whom we need not be afraid to show ourselves as we really are, warts and all. But we have become so complicated that we ourselves hardly know which are the warts and which are the beauty spots! It is also true that lovers in the first ecstasy of union imagine that they know each other through and through, even as they imagine the other to be perfect.

I have come to realize that although I know my husband of many, many years far better than anyone else, I still do not know him as well as God alone knows him; as possibly he knows himself. And I believe this is true of all of us.

Reflections on Yourself

So now I am asking you to try to unravel some of the mystery that is you. It may be as well to begin by putting yourself before God. You have been looking at God; now it is God's turn to look at you! You can be sure that God knows you better than you know yourself. In Psalm 44 we read:

> Had we forgotten your name, O God,
> or stretched out our hands to another god,
> would you not have found this out,
> you who know the secrets of the heart? (Ps. 44:21-22)

But the psalm that I hope you will find helpful now is arguably the most fascinating of all 150 psalms. It is the song of someone like you, humbling yourself before God, aware of God's intimate knowledge of and care for each of us. Please read these words slowly, applying them to yourself:

> O Lord, you search me and you know me,
> you know my resting and my rising,
> you discern my purpose from afar.
> You mark when I walk or lie down,
> all my ways lie open to you.
>
> Before ever a word is on my tongue
> you know it, O Lord, through and through.
> Behind and before you besiege me,
> your hand ever laid upon me.
> Too wonderful for me, this knowledge,
> too high, beyond my reach.
>
> O where can I go from your spirit,
> or where can I flee from your face?
> If I climb the heavens you are there.
> If I lie in the grave, you are there.
>
> If I take the wings of the dawn
> and dwell at the sea's furthest end,
> even there your hand would lead me,
> your right hand would hold me fast.

If I say, "Let the darkness hide me
and the light around me be night,"
even darkness is not dark for you
and the night is as clear as the day.
For it was you who created my being,
knit me together in my mother's womb.
I thank you for the wonder of my being,
for the wonders of all your creation.

Already you knew my soul,
my body held no secret from you
when I was being fashioned in secret
and molded in the depths of the earth.

O search me, my God, and know my heart.
O test me and know my thoughts.
See that I follow not the wrong path
and lead me in the path of life eternal. (Ps. 139:1-15, 23-24)

SILENCE

So you, and I, and everyone stand stripped and naked
before God. With God there can be no pretense. Let us not
pretend with ourselves either, but try to see with clear eyes
what we are really like. Try to remove some of your "outer
garment," that is, the "you" that you show to the world
and perhaps believe to be your self.

You may find it more comfortable to think of yourself
as standing not before God the Father but before Jesus.
Once, when I was giving a retreat, I invited the young
people to think of themselves as Mary Magdalene by the
empty tomb in the garden, and to imagine how it felt to
be her. Here is the Gospel story:

Meanwhile Mary stayed outside near the tomb, weeping.
Then, still weeping, she stooped to look inside, and saw
two angels in white sitting where the body of Jesus had
been, one at the head, the other at the feet. They said,

"Woman, why are you weeping?" "They have taken my Lord away," she replied, "and I don't know where they have put him." As she said this she turned round and saw Jesus standing there, though she did not recognize him. Jesus said, "Woman, why are you weeping? Who are you looking for?" Supposing him to be the gardener, she said, "Sir, if you have taken him away, tell me where you have put him, and I will go and remove him." Jesus said, "Mary!" She knew him then and said to him in Hebrew, "Rabbuni!"— which means Master. (John 20:11-16)

Here are two of the responses from the retreatants:

I was in such a state of panic—like a mad thing running round in circles. Where was his body? Where could he be? There was no one to ask.

The garden was so still in the early morning, still and quiet, and as I afterwards realized, beautiful.

I ran this way and that, and at last to my relief I saw a man. "The gardener"—was my immediate thought—he might know something! I called to him in desperation: "Oh, tell me, have you seen my Lord? Where have you put him?"

The man said nothing. I had run up to him now, wringing my hands, frantic, so obsessed with my own misery that I didn't really see.

Then he spoke.

He said, "Mary."

My name.

And I knew.

I have heard him say my name.
I have heard him say "Rosamund."
I was not expecting him
but he was waiting for me.
I realize now he has been saying my name since birth,
but till now, I never heard.
And it has changed my life,

for his word affirms
all that I have been, all I am and all I will be!

So now, with the clear gaze of God upon you, look into your own heart. If you find it useful, write down your feelings.

To help you, I will tell you what happened to me when I tried to do this. I honestly thought I was quite a nice person. I was always sympathetic, such a good listener, doing kindnesses all over the place to all sorts of people. And all sorts of people seemed to think I was nice too. It was only when I paused to take stock that I realized that all was not quite what it seemed. I saw that very often I was so nice and kind and sympathetic not for love of God or even of the people I was helping, but for love of myself. You see, I wanted very much to be liked and I had found a successful way to achieve this.

When I came to this realization I was dismayed and ashamed. Then I remembered not only the mercy but also the understanding of God. I tried to develop my own understanding of myself a little further. I began to see that I had a tremendous, compelling *need* to be liked, and that this need in turn was rooted in the experience of rejection.

I was still ashamed, especially as I now saw how false my behavior had been, but I no longer thought of myself as a heinous sinner, and I realized that there are a great many other people who share this weakness of mine.

As soon as I was able to see the un-Christlike motives behind my seemingly Christian actions, I made up my mind to change. I knew that I would not be capable of a sudden and complete reversal of my behavior, but, because I understood how gentle our God is with us, I was able to be gentle with myself; and slowly, slowly, through the Holy Spirit, I began to change not only my outward behavior but also my inner self. I am not sure whether people like me more or less, but the great thing is, I do not really mind.

I have written this as an example in the hope of helping you. Each of us is unique, and you may well find that your experience of self-discovery is completely different from mine. Such self-discovery is a sort of journey, and it may well take a lifetime to complete. In some sense it is a journey backward to the innocence and transparency of childhood.

It may also help to ask yourself some questions, and to write the answers in your notebook.

First think about your *body:*

- What is your state of health?
- Do you worry about your health?
- Do you put off going to the doctor?
- Do you get enough exercise?
- Do you eat the sort of food that is good for you?
- Do you smoke or eat too much?
- Are you overweight or underweight?
- Are you happy with your sexuality?

Your *mind:*

- Do you try to broaden your knowledge?
- Do you take an interest in "serious" topics?
- Are you concerned about politics?
- Are you concerned about social issues?
- Are you concerned about religion?
- Have you tried to sort out your own prejudices?
- What *are* your prejudices?
- Are you creative in any way?
- Do you appreciate creativity in others, for example: music, poetry, painting, sculpture, embroidery?
- Do you watch, listen to, or read things you know to be "rubbish"?

Your *emotions:*

- Are you moody?
- Do you get angry easily?
- Are you usually cheerful?
- Are you quite often mildly depressed?
- Are you sometimes deeply depressed?
- Are you an enthusiastic person?
- Are you easily bored?
- Do you bottle up your emotions?
- Do you suffer from anxiety?

When you have answered all these questions and perhaps added some more comments on yourself, write a thumbnail sketch of your character, something like this imaginary one:

> I am in good health, slightly overweight, and I do not get enough exercise. I take an interest in religion and social issues but I hate politics. I thought I was not prejudiced at all but when I thought about it I had to admit that I am something of a snob. I love music, but I seldom read poetry and never visit art galleries. I like watching soap operas on television and reading detective stories and I am not sure that I would agree that these things are rubbish. I am never bored and sometimes I become extremely enthusiastic.

What else can you say about yourself to add to this picture? Perhaps something like this: I am lazy. I love to stay in bed in the morning. I am greedy, especially when it comes to sweet things. I am vain—I spend too much time on my looks. I am honest. I think I am generous. I care about justice. I worry nearly all the time.

It is good to take a clear honest look at yourself, but take care that you are not too judgmental. It is not "wrong" not to visit art galleries or to go to concerts, and arguably it is sometimes "right" to relax and enjoy the sort of books and programs that do nothing to stimulate the mind. When you have thought about yourself you may want to change in some ways, but I hope you will also be happy to accept most of what you discover about yourself. Do not expect to be an angel: be glad that you are human!

In the list of questions, I deliberately divided the areas into body, mind, and feelings. I might have also included "spirit" as a heading. Our souls, bodies, minds and hearts (emotions) are interdependent, closely and powerfully related to one another. It is interesting, and to some of us actually surprising, how un-separate these parts of ourselves are in reality. This came home to me vividly not so long ago.

I suddenly became aware that I was having quite a number of minor ailments: a sore throat, mouth ulcers, frequent colds, daily headaches. I was getting plenty of exercise and eating healthy food. I simply could not understand it. It hardly seemed worth going to the doctor, but one day when I woke with a streaming cold for the umpteenth time I made an appointment to see her.

To my surprise, instead of examining me, she asked if I was worrying about anything. I poured out my anxiety over one of my children who was in serious trouble. Apparently all my physical ailments were the direct result of the state of my mind and heart.

Now you need some time in silence—a space to take a long honest look at the person you are. Do you think you are very far from the person God wants you to be?

Ask yourself what you are most afraid of, what you long for, what you think about most, what motivates you, and how you relate to others. You could write the answers in your notebook.

SILENCE

At the beginning of this day I asked you to try to let go of your personal problems. Now I am going to ask you to face them. Suppose you have been trying faithfully to do as I suggest. My guess is that, especially in this particular chapter, where you have been asked to think about yourself, your degree of enthusiasm will depend on how much you are burdened by personal worries.

Suppose someone is in a marital crisis. Let us say there is a husband who after a happy and successful marriage of several years, has suddenly fallen in love with another woman. Such a man, if he has taken a day away to sort himself out, will have great difficulty in concentrating his thoughts on anything other than his overriding dilemma. Even if he has managed to give a considerable time to reflection on God, when it comes to looking at himself there will be only one question on his mind: should he leave his wife or not?

Someone else may have just lost her job. Another person may be recently bereaved, mourning the death of someone they cannot bear to live without. Someone may be trying to gather the courage to take a test for HIV.

Problems like these are enormous, overwhelming for the people concerned. We cannot hand them over to the Lord and forget them, because for the moment at least they are such a huge part of who we are. We cannot hand them to God and forget about them, but we can ask God to come in, to be there with us. We can share our pain, our confusion, our bitterness, our anger, with God. We can rage and cry in God's presence without fear of rejection. We may not find any answers, but there is a chance that we may receive a reassuring touch from the one who does care, however messy, sinful, or hopeless the situation may be.

Joyce Huggett tells us how a friend of hers, who was in the depths of despair, described a vision she had.

She was married to a pastor but had indulged in an affair with a married man. Eventually, realization dawned that she had reached a crossroads. Either she must leave her husband and children and cause untold hurt to numerous people, or she must give up her love. She chose the latter.

Having repented of the illicit love affair, she wandered into the woods to think and to pray. As she continued to pour out the bitterness of her soul to God, she described her life to him as nothing more than fragments of her former self. While she stood silent and still before God, into her mind came a picture of the fragments she had described: they littered the ground like so many pieces of red clay. As she gazed at the broken vessel representing her life, into the picture came Jesus. She saw the tenderness of his face and observed the sensitivity of his fingers as he stooped down and started to turn over all those forlorn fragments. "Suddenly he started to piece them together," she told me. "He assured me that, though the vessel was a mess, every tiny piece of the pot was precious. I watched the skill with which he put the pieces together again. He recreated the vessel. He showed me that it would be even more useful. Then he glazed it and held it up for me to see. I couldn't see a single sign of the joints where the cracked parts had been pressed back together."[3]

Not all of us, when our lives are broken, can experience such a vision of healing. Indeed, perhaps most of us carry the scars left by the experience of deep unhappiness to the end of our lives. But we can all hold our brokenness before the one who loves us beyond all loving.

It may be that, at this time, you are not weighed down with troubles of this magnitude. Even so, it is unlikely that you will be entirely problem-free. Can you, in God's presence, face such problems squarely; look them in the eye? They will probably not disappear or be solved, but the odds are that they will diminish. When we look at things with God, we receive a sense of proportion.

I am looking at my own minor problems. First, I live so far from all my children. Four of my five grandchildren live in another country. One of my sons has disappeared for the moment. These things make me sad, but I realize that in almost every case the children have far bigger problems than any of mine. I think that all of them, including the missing one, genuinely love me, and this is a gift beyond price.

Second, my migraines. They are occurring day after day now, almost every day. They are painful and wearing, and try as I might, I cannot discover what causes them. They stop me from reading, writing, watching television, making plans. Sometimes I feel upset and angry and afraid that they will never end.

But when I sit quietly and think about this I realize that I am not so much cursed by the migraines as blessed. I am not suffering from cancer or heart trouble or recurring strokes or a progressive disease. The pain is bearable and does not last for long. Some days the headaches are in remission and that I appreciate as I appreciate sunshine after rain.

Third, I have recently undertaken to be a bereavement counselor. This frightens me, in case I let the bereaved person down instead of helping her. But I see now that this is foolish, I am just timid and lacking in confidence. She is the one who matters in this situation.

Perhaps it is worth mentioning here that just after I had written this my telephone rang. It was someone I hardly knew at all, who had heard about my migraines and was offering me helpful advice. So often *this* is the way our God works: through the kindness of others.

It is very likely that you will have similar problems. Imagine that you are sitting side by side with God, or with Jesus if that is easier for you. Tell him about your anxieties and try to see them through his eyes.

You have been considering your character and your problems. Now I would like to suggest that you think about your gifts. Your first reaction may be, "I haven't got any," in which case I ask you to think a little further.

In the first place there are the free gifts that come from God, gifts in the sense of presents rather than talents. I am aware as I write this that some of us are not as richly blessed as others. We are all born equal in the sight of God.

We are all loved equally by God, but we have only to look around us to see how differently we are endowed. If we are blind we do not have the gift of sunrise, sunset, moonlight, starlight, and a thousand other beautiful sights. If we are deaf we do not have the gift of music or bird song or children's laughter or the voice of a lover.

But today, at this time, you are thinking about what God has given *you*. Count your blessings, write them down in your notebook, and you will find that it is beginning to fill fast. I will just begin my own list to give you some ideas:

- my husband
- my children
- my grandchildren
- my home
- my health
- my enjoyment of life
- color
- daffodils
- clouds
- Mozart
- radio
- books
- friends

These are not in any special order—indeed my friends are of great importance to me. But I can see already that "my cup runneth over," as it says in the King James Version of Psalm 23.

The other sort of gifts we receive from God are our own talents, and here you are even more likely to say "But I haven't got any!" This is probably false humility, or simply not realizing what talents God has given you.

- Can you smile?
- Can you listen?
- Can you be gentle?
- Can you be strong?

Well, yes, you may reluctantly admit, but then, so can everybody else. Don't you believe it. If you can use these talents well, not only are you talented, but you have gifts of great value. There are some people who are not gifted in any obvious way because of illness or disability. But there are many more who have gifts that they fail to use because they are not aware of them or think they are not good enough or are just plain shy.

Since my husband is one such, he may not be too pleased when I tell you that he has a fine singing voice. Can you guess how long it took him to realize this? He was sixty-three when he was finally cajoled into joining a choir!

In thinking about ourselves it is important to remember the great commandments of Jesus.

"You must love the Lord your God with all your heart, with all your soul, with all your strength, and with all your mind, and your neighbor as yourself." (Luke 10:27)

We are not very good at obeying the last part of this command. Loving ourselves does not come easily. And you may feel this even more keenly after you have taken a good look at yourself. Damian Lundy understands this very well. He writes:

We have grown up in a painful world; we are bruised and scarred by the anger, sarcasm, impatience and selfishness of others, to which we have contributed amply. Sometimes we hate ourselves because we fail to measure up to the demands made of us by parents, teachers, friends, or the demands we make of ourselves. We never *deserve* 100 percent but we always demand it—which makes us, and everybody, *failures*. We're under constant pressure, much of it from within ourselves, from our guilt, fears, weakness and shame. Think of *your* fears, your guilt: do not run from them—*face them*. Imagine you are gathering them into a bundle. *Name* your worries and anxieties, and *one by one*, throw them into the bundle.

113

Now bring your bundle to Christ. Don't be afraid—he is the divine rubbish-collector, who takes away the sins of all the world. Throw your rubbish into his grave. . . . The darkness swallows it. Watch it disappear. The grave is empty because Christ is risen: he has destroyed death, sin, guilt, shame, darkness, including your guilty secrets, your *fears*. He offers you complete forgiveness, new life, true healing. Thank him for his love and for the joy, peace, courage and inner freedom he has given you.[4]

Can you try to do as Damian suggests now?

Sometimes it is very hard to believe that we are lovable, acceptable even, to others. Most of us have a low level of self-esteem. Even those people who seem full of self-importance often turn out to be the ones who are most insecure underneath.

Unless we *can* feel accepted and loved by others, it is almost impossible for us to love ourselves. But there is always hope. Some psychologists believed that if a child was unloved during his or her first years, he or she would have no chance of experiencing love—of either giving or receiving it. But more recently there seems to be the possibility that through faithful, sensitive loving over a long period, even the loveless man or woman can come alive and begin to see his or her own worth. That is one reason why for all of us, whether or not we grew up in a loving family, good friends are of immeasurable value, because they help to sustain us in our belief in ourselves as worthwhile, lovable human beings.

Peter van Breemen writes perceptively about this:

One of the deepest needs of the human heart is the need to be appreciated. Every human being craves to be accepted for what he is. . . . When I am not accepted, then something in me is broken. A baby who is not accepted is ruined at the roots of his existence. . . . Acceptance means that the people with whom I live give me a feeling of self-respect, a feeling that I am worthwhile. They are happy that I am who I am.

Acceptance means that I am happy to be myself. . . . I do not have to be the person I am not. Neither am I locked in by my past or present. Rather I am given room to unfold, to outgrow the mistakes of the past. . . . When a person is appreciated for what he *does*, he is not unique; someone else can do the work perhaps even better than he. But when a person is loved for what he *is*, then he becomes a unique and irreplaceable personality. I need that acceptance in order to be myself. When I am not accepted, I am a nobody. I cannot come to fulfillment. An accepted person is a happy person because he is opened up, because he can grow.[5]

I would like to ask you to do something very simple: to hold your head high as a sign that you accept yourself as someone worthy of love. Hold your head high, and smile in recognition of the joyous challenge of life.

Now you may like to say this prayer:

I thank thee, Lord, for knowing me better than I know myself, and for letting me know myself better than others know me.[6]

Can you draw a symbol of yourself, as you feel now?

Supper

It is time for supper, or a break if you have already eaten. Here is a grace you may like to say:

Dear Lord,
my heart is full of thanks
for all your blessings.
I thank you for this food,
for the good earth, the sunshine, and the rain
and for all those whose work has been part
of the making of my food.
I thank you for the people in my life,
and most of all, for your love. Amen.

CHAPTER 7

Night

Looking Outward
Looking Ahead
A Letter from God
Winding Down

"Then the King will say to those on his right hand, 'Come, you whom my Father has blessed, take for your heritage the kingdom prepared for you since the foundation of the world. For I was hungry and you gave me food; I was thirsty and you gave me drink; I was a stranger and you made me welcome; naked and you clothed me, sick and you visited me, in prison and you came to see me.' Then the virtuous will say to him in reply, 'Lord, when did we see you hungry and feed you; or thirsty and give you drink? When did we see you a stranger and make you welcome; naked and clothe you; sick or in prison and go to see you?' And the King will answer, 'I tell you solemnly, in so far as you did this to one of the least of these brothers of mine, you did it to me.'" (Matt. 25:34-40)

Now you are drawing toward the end of the day. You may be feeling tired. You may be longing to get home, to be back in your own sitting room watching television. Or you may wish you could stay, and experience many more days like this.

However you are feeling, these last few hours of the day will be for the most part free for you to do whatever you choose. But before you relax there are one or two things I would like you to consider. You have been looking at God and then at yourself. In this last part of the day I would like you to look at your neighbor, the one you are asked by Jesus to love as yourself.

Looking Outward

Just who *is* your neighbor? He or she is anyone at all whose life touches yours. They could be family, friends, literally the people next door or in your street, people whose lives you hear about in the media. Spend some time now thinking about those who are closest to you, their hopes and fears, sorrows and joys. Particularly think of anyone who is in special need, who may be glad of your interest and compassion. To suffer pain alongside those we love is one of the greatest callings of Christ's followers.

Yesterday I was spending the day at home. In the morning I listened to a phone-in radio program. The subject was euthanasia. It was intended to be a discussion of the rights and wrongs of "mercy killing," but as it turned out many of the callers were simply describing their personal experiences of the harrowing deaths of people they had loved.

I was distressed, as all listeners must have been, to hear not only of the pain and misery of the dying, but of the intense grief of those who had to watch them die. Somehow, listening to the radio, without any knowledge of the callers, without having myself experienced any of this particular kind of suffering, I felt drawn, to some very small degree, into their sorrow. There is a temptation to switch off the radio, to say, "I don't want to know," but I felt a compulsion to go on listening and to lift all those people to God. Later in the day I watched a television program called: "Why Blame the Mother?" It was about the mothers of rapists and murderers. It showed clearly how these women felt. I was certainly moved to pity but even though I have myself had the unhappy experience of visiting my son in prison, I realized it was beyond my imagining to comprehend what those mothers have to go through.

Then I saw that later in the evening of the same day there was to be a John Pilger film about East Timor. I had some idea what it would be like and I thought, "Can I take any more?" But in the end I decided to watch it because I greatly admire the courage of John Pilger, and I felt that I should learn the truth about what happened and is still happening in that distant country.

The film was horrific. I was shocked and appalled by the hideous brutality of the Indonesian soldiers and even more by the hypocrisy and greed of some of the diplomats and politicians. Jesus said, "Do not judge, and you will not be judged" (Matt. 7:1) but it is difficult to restrain one's feeling of anger at the sight of so much inhumanity.

So I spent a good deal of yesterday learning about the suffering of others, and trying to respond to it. But I am left wondering what use is my compassion, my caring, my increased awareness to all these of my brothers and sisters who have had to endure so much.

I know only too well that I, and all of us, share some guilt for these dreadful happenings, and all of us have the responsibility to be in some way involved with the victims in our society, by prayer, by spreading awareness, and where possible, by giving money. There is a moving modern hymn, which asks for God's mercy on us for our corporate sin in allowing our world to become as it is:

> Look around you, can you see?
> Times are troubled, people grieve.
> See the violence, feel the hardness,
> all my people, weep with me.
> Kyrie eleison, Kyrie eleison, Kyrie eleison.[1]

I feel discouraged and sad that I can do almost nothing; and yet I believe that those people (of whom I hope I am one), who hold the values of the gospel and struggle to follow the example and teachings of Jesus, must be a power for pity and mercy and justice in our world.

There is a temptation for us Christians to stay within our cozy church communities, closing our eyes to other traditions and other faiths, shutting out thoughts of the hopeless mass of suffering people who are somewhere "out there," but whose lives do not impinge on ours unless we let them.

As Christians we *have* to let them. We have to hear the cry of the poor and wipe the tears of those who grieve. Unless we are concerned for justice we are not worthy to bear the name of Christian. I remember reading a book by Henri Nouwen, Donald McNeill, and Douglas Morrison. It is called, simply, *Compassion*. In the epilogue the authors recount how they met a man called Joel Filártiga, a medical doctor and artist in Paraguay whose seventeen-year-old son had been tortured and killed. They write:

> The more we heard about Joel, the more we began to realize what compassion is. It is hard work; it is crying out with those in pain; it is tending the wounds of the poor and caring for their lives; it is defending the weak and indignantly accusing those who violate their humanity; it is joining with the oppressed in their struggle for justice; it is pleading for help, with all possible means, from any person who has ears to hear and eyes to see. In short, it is a willingness to lay down our lives for our friends.[2]

SILENCE

It is important too to keep a sense of proportion. When we look around us we see not only sorrow, but happiness too. We should take care that we are not overwhelmed by the tragedies around us. We must remember that there is joy in abundance: in love, in friendship, in marriage, birth, and even sometimes in old age! There is joy in nature, and sport and sex and song and laughter. Jesus wants us to experience joy. He said:

> If you keep my commandments
> you will remain in my love,
> just as I have kept my Father's commandments
> and remain in his love.
> I have told you this
> so that my own joy may be in you
> and your joy be complete. (John 15:10-11)

Later in the same Gospel, shortly before his death, Jesus said:

> A woman in childbirth suffers,
> because her time has come;
> but when she has given birth to the child she forgets the
>   suffering
> in her joy that a man has been born into the world.
> So it is with you: you are sad now,
> but I shall see you again, and your hearts will be full of joy,
> and that joy no one shall take from you. (John 16:21-22)

And Paul, in his Letter to the Philippians, gives them a prescription for joy that is appropriate for us too:

> I want you to be happy, always happy in the Lord; I repeat, what I want is your happiness. Let your tolerance be evident to everyone: the Lord is very near. There is no need to worry; but if there is anything you need, pray for it, asking God for it with prayer and thanksgiving, and that peace of God, which is so much greater than we can understand, will guard your hearts and your thoughts, in Christ Jesus. Finally, brothers, fill your minds with everything that is true, everything that is noble, everything that is good and pure, everything that we love and honor, and

everything that can be thought virtuous or worthy of praise. (Phil. 4:4-8)

During this day you have looked at God: God the Father, God the Son, God the Holy Spirit, and you have looked at Jesus Christ. You have looked inward, and just now you were looking outward and around you.

Give yourself a space of silence now and try to make a cohesion of your day.

SILENCE

Looking Ahead

After your time of silence, begin to think of tomorrow. How will you be when you wake up? Refreshed, changed, challenged? Resolved to treat others differently and look carefully at your attitudes? Perhaps you have learned the valuable lesson of accepting your own limitations. Are you willing to try to work out what are God's hopes and desires for you? Will you seek some stillness, tomorrow and every day after, some time to be alone, in silence with God? Will you already look forward to another day like this, like this one, but different? Do you feel that you are a step nearer the kingdom of God?

It is very difficult for us to grasp what exactly Jesus means by "the kingdom." Because of our limited experience and vision, we cannot fully understand such concepts as "eternity" and "kingdom."

The poet R. S. Thomas imagined the kingdom like this:

> It's a long way off but inside it
> There are quite different things going on:
> Festivals at which the poor man
> Is king and the consumptive is
> Healed; mirrors in which the blind look
> At themselves and love looks at them

Back; and industry is for mending
The bent bones and the minds fractured
By life. It's a long way off, but to get
There takes no time and admission
Is free, if you will purge yourself
Of desire, and present yourself with
Your need only and the simple offering
Of your faith, green as a leaf.[3]

I hope you have found God today, or felt closer to him. Where do you think you will find God tomorrow, and the next day, and during the rest of your life? You may feel like the writer of this poem:

Oh where will I find him,
The one who is my God?
In the dim mystery of a great cathedral
Where glorious arches leap to praise him?
In the plain quiet of the convent chapel
Where simplicity does him honour?
Up and away in the green hills
Under a shining sky
With flowers under my feet
And a soft wind caressing me?
Or will I find him
Down, down below
In the gutter,
On the floor of an overcrowded hospital
Among the wounded and the hurting and the longing?
Where will I find my God?

What is it that above all you seek from life?

- Power?
- Success?
- Security?
- The respect and love of others?
- Justice *for* others?
- Happiness?

Perhaps what each of us ultimately seeks, beyond all of these things, is peace, because when we have found what we are driven to seek, we believe that our minds and our hearts will be at peace. Yet peace itself is not too simple a concept.

The poet Brian Wren writes movingly in his poem "Say 'No' to Peace":

> Say "no" to peace if what they mean by peace
> is the quiet misery of hunger,
> the frozen stillness of fear,
> the silence of broken spirits,
> the unborn hopes of the oppressed.
>
> Tell them that peace is the shouting of children at play,
> the babble of tongues set free,
> the thunder of dancing feet,
> and a father's voice singing love.
>
> Say "no" to peace if what they mean by peace
> is the rampart of gleaming missiles,
> the arming of distant wars,
> money at ease in its castle
> and grateful poor at the gate.
>
> Tell them that peace is the hauling down of flags,
> the forging of guns into ploughs,
> the giving of fields to the landless,
> and hunger a fading dream.[4]

As long as we are concerned for all those who cannot be at peace, we are not able ourselves to receive in its fullness the gift that Christ left behind for us:

> Peace I bequeath to you,
> my own peace I give you,
> a peace the world cannot give, this is my gift to you.
> (John 14:27)

123

It has become almost a truism to say of peace, "Let it begin with me," and yet it is a profound truth. We will never become effective peacemakers until we are peaceful people, gentle, accepting, listening people, aware of conflict, brave enough to face confrontation, but a source of assurance and affirmation to others.

A Letter from God

And now I am going to suggest that you do something very difficult indeed. Earlier in the day I asked you to write a letter to God. Now I want you to write a letter to yourself *from* God. This is not some sort of blasphemy or an attempt to achieve the impossible, to get into the mind of God. It is simply a way of trying to see yourself as God sees you, and to see this day as God sees it.

If you are one of those people who found it impossible to write a letter *to* God, then you will really be digging your heels in now. And yet, in some ways, this one is easier. It should also be of greater value, bringing together your reflections on what this day has meant and will mean, for you.

The letter—if you can bring yourself to write it, will be the last thing you enter in your notebook today. I would like you to look on the notebook as something of real worth, something to keep not only in remembrance of this day, but to refresh and encourage you when there is need.

Winding Down

As you go to bed this night, I pray this blessing for you:

The LORD bless you and keep you;
the LORD make his face to shine upon you, and be gracious
    to you;
the LORD lift up his countenance upon you, and give you
    peace. (Num. 6:24-26 NRSV)

In the introduction to this book, you were asked to ponder the first two verses of Psalm 63. You may like to reflect on the third verse the last thing at night on this day:

> On my bed I remember you,
> On you I muse through the night
> for you have been my help;
> in the shadow of your wings I rejoice.
> My soul clings to you;
> your right hand holds me fast. (Ps. 63:3)

You have been musing all through this day, so I hope you will not be musing through the night! Good night and God bless you.

Notes

Introduction

1. Gerard Manley Hopkins, "Heaven-Haven," *The Poems of Gerard Manley Hopkins*, ed. W. H. Gardner and Norman H. MacKenzie (New York: Oxford University Press, 1970).

1. Dawn

1. C. Day Lewis, "Walking Away" from *The Complete Poems of C. Day Lewis*, ed. Jill Balcon (Stanford University Press, 1992).
2. John Greenleaf Whittier, "Dear Lord and Father of Mankind," *The United Methodist Hymnal* (Nashville: The United Methodist Publishing House, 1989), no. 358.
3. Jim Cotter, *Towards the City* (Cairns Publications, 1993) is a version of Psalms 101–50.
4. William Wordsworth, "She Dwelt Among the Untrodden Ways," *The Oxford Book of English Verse* (New York: Oxford University Press, n.d.), pp. 485-86.
5. Thich Nhat Hanh, *Our Appointment with Life: The Buddha's Teaching on Living in the Present* (Berkeley: Calif.: Parallax Press, 1990).

2. Early Morning

1. *Fioretti of St. Francis*, anonymous, 1370.

3. Late Morning

1. William Wordsworth, "Ode to Duty," *The Oxford Book of English Verse* (New York: Oxford University Press, n.d.), pp. 494-95.
2. Wordsworth, "Daffodils," *The Oxford Book of English Verse*, pp. 493-94.

3. *Hildegard of Bingen*, eds. F. Bowie and O. Davies (London: SPCK, 1990).

4. Julian of Norwich, *Revelations of Divine Love*, ed. Clifton Wolters (New York: Viking Penguin, 1982).

5. From the Mass for Pentecost Sunday in *The Sunday Missal* (San Francisco: Collins, 1984).

6. Teresa of Avila, *Complete Works*, trans. E. A. Peers (Kansas City, Mo.: Sheed and Ward, 1982).

7. Caryll Houselander, "The Young Man" in T. H. Parker and F. J. Teskey, *Let There Be God.*

8. Thomas Batty, *Account of Experiences with the Indians* (1873).

9. See note 5 above.

10. See note 5 above.

4. Early Afternoon

1. Charles Wesley, "Gentle Jesus, Meek and Mild" from *Hymns and Sacred Poems* (1742).

2. Cecil Frances Alexander, "Once in Royal David's City," *The United Methodist Hymnal* (Nashville: The United Methodist Publishing House, 1989), no. 250.

3. Caryll Houselander, "God Abides in Man" in Parker and Teskey, *Let There Be God.*

5. Late Afternoon

1. Tokio Megashie.

2. Poem by Anthea Dove.

6. Evening

1. This is an anonymous inscription on the temple of Apollo at Delphi.

2. *The Cloud of Unknowing and Other Works*, trans. Clifton Wolters (New York: Viking Penguin, 1978).

3. Joyce Huggett, *Listening to God* (London: Hodder & Stoughton, 1986).

4. Damian Lundy, *To Grow in Christ* (Kevin Mayhew, 1980).

5. Peter G. van Breemen, *As Bread That Is Broken* (Denville, N.J.: Dimension Books, 1974).

6. Abu Bekr (died A.D. 634).

7. Night

1. Jodi Page Clarke, "Kyrie Eleison," *Songs of the Spirit 2* (Kevin Mayhew, 1981).
2. Henri Nouwen, Donald McNeill, and Douglas Morrison, *Compassion* (DLT, 1982).
3. R. S. Thomas, "The Kingdom" from *Later Poems* (New York: Macmillan, 1983).
4. Brian Wren, "Say 'No' to Peace," *Praising a Mystery* (Sebastopol, Calif.: Wild Goose, 1986).